HIDDEN
HISTORY
of Horse Racing in
KENTUCKY

Foster Ockerman Jr.

THE
History
PRESS

D1453466

Published by The History Press
Charleston, SC
www.historypress.com

Copyright © 2019 by Foster Ockerman Jr.
All rights reserved

Front cover: Keeneland Library.
Back cover: Lexington History Museum, Inc.; *inset*: Bill Straus.

First published 2019

Manufactured in the United States

ISBN 9781467138949

Library of Congress Control Number: 2018963657

This book is dedicated to our grandson, Michael Foster Helsby,
in the hope that he comes to love history as much as his grandfather.

Contents

ACKNOWLEDGEMENTS

This has been an intriguing detective hunt. My thanks go to Sarah Hubbard, director of the Kentucky Room and her staff at the Lexington Public Library; Becky Ryan, director of the library, and her staff at the Keeneland Association Library—a very beautiful place to conduct research; Eric Brooks, curator at Ashland, Henry Clay's home; Chris Goodletter, curator at the Kentucky Derby Museum; local historian Bill Ambrose (especially for sharing some not-yet-published material); Patrick Lewis of the Kentucky Historical Society; Aaron Genton at Shaker Village of Pleasant Hill; the Adelin Wichman estate for permission to use her portraits of African American jockeys; and Andy Mead and Pace Emmons for taking photographs of the portraits at what proved to be difficult angles and the technical prowess to adjust for the angles; as well as Fran Taylor and Wendy Bright. I want to acknowledge the encouragement of the late Dr. Ken Kinghorn, professor of church history and a United Methodist historian, and his regular question: "Well, what did you write this week?" I also thank my wife, Martina, for allowing me to do a forced occupation of the dining-room table with books stacked all about while I was writing.

A portion of the sales proceeds of this book benefit the Lexington History Museum, Inc.

Introduction

A ccording to the 2012 Kentucky Equine Survey, conducted by the University of Kentucky, the equine industry in Kentucky generated a total economic impact of almost $3 billion and created more than 40,000 jobs in the year prior to the survey. There were about 54,000 thoroughbred horses, 42,000 quarter horses, 36,000 Tennessee walking horses, 14,000 saddlebreds, 9,500 standardbreds and 12,500 Kentucky mountain horse breeds as well as ponies, draft horses, Arabians and other breeds. In the total were almost 4,000 breeding stallions. Lexington-Fayette County has the most horses, with some 89,000, followed by Bourbon, Woodford and Scott Counties, all in the central Bluegrass Region.

This book digs into history to find out how it all started. Here you will find that local racetracks once were almost as prevalent as high school football fields, that horse races were run on the main streets of early towns, that Henry Clay was as good a horse breeder as he was a politician and that African American jockeys were our country's first professional athletes, among other tidbits of equine history.

THE HISTORY OF THE HORSE

B efore there can be a history of horse racing, there must first be a horse to race. In Kentucky, at least, children were taught in elementary school that horses were first brought to the Americas by the Spanish conquistadors in the fifteenth century, and that escaped or abandoned horses went wild and spread into North America, where the native Indians adapted them to use.

While the latter part of that history is true, the Spanish did not *first* introduce horses here. In fact, the earliest animal that would evolve into the modern horse originated in North America.[1]

The first little horse was *Hyracotherium* or *Eohippus* ("dawn horse"), which lived fifty-five to forty-five million years ago in central North America. It stood between ten and seventeen inches tall at the shoulder with four toes on its front legs and three toes on its hind legs. This configuration helped keep Eohippus from sinking into the swampy condition of the land at that time and evade predators.[2] Evidence of this animal has been found in Utah and Wyoming.[3]

Little *Eohippus* evolved into *Mesohippus*, now growing up to forty inches tall at the shoulder and possessing longer legs.[4] It lived roughly thirty-seven to thirty-two million years ago. Changes in the climate and geography drove the physical changes in this early horse as the swamps had turned into soft ground. The outside toes were smaller, while the middle toe became larger.[5]

Next came *Pliohippus* or *Equus*, in the Pleistocene epoch; it would be recognized today as a horse.[6] This period was twelve to six million years ago.

The flanking toes had further receded and the center toe had evolved into a hoof. Teeth and legs resemble the modern horse, and *Equus* had evolved into a faster runner. It spread into South America and across the land bridge at the Bering Strait into Asia, Europe and eventually Africa.[7]

For reasons not yet known, *Equus* became extinct in the Americas between eight thousand and ten thousand years ago.[8]

Equus evolved into the modern horse in Central Asia. There, horses changed in use from sources of food to transportation, both pulling loads and as personal conveyance.[9]

Finally, the horse came full circle and was returned to the Americas with Hernán Cortéz on his excursion to Mexico in 1519.[10] The first recorded horse brought to colonial America by the English was to Jamestown in 1610, three years after settlement. By 1620, horses were fairly common in the Virginia colony, although used primarily as working beasts, not for pleasure or sport.[11]

Whether the first horse race started with a wager, a challenge or an inspired flight from danger is lost in the mists of history. Horse racing is one of the oldest sports, and its core concept has never changed: the horse that gets to the finish first wins![12]

What is clear is that once the basic tenets of how to break, train and ride a horse were worked out, military leaders were quick to take advantage of the escalation in weapons delivery the horse produced. The Assyrians, Egyptians, Mongols and other ancient peoples used chariots in battle. Chariot races were run in the Greek Olympics in 610 BC and are featured in Homer's *Illiad*.[13] What today is called a "parting shot," a verbal insult cast over the shoulder as the speaker leaves a room or stage, has its origin in a military tactic of the Parthians, an ancient Iranian culture. They perfected the shooting of an arrow at full gallop while turned around on the back of the horse. An enemy would think the Parthian cavalry was retreating and charge, only to meet a wall of arrows as the horsemen attacked "in reverse." This required tremendous skill on the part of the rider, as the stirrup had not been invented and the rider commanded his horse solely with knee pressure while his head and hands were occupied shooting his bow.[14]

The Romans, of course, followed, and many nobles had large stables of horses.[15] Romans raced both chariots and individually mounted horses.[16] Even the modern sport of eventing, commonly called a Three Day Event, arose from military use of the horse in battle in the nineteenth century.[17] The first day is dressage, a kind of equine ballet in which rider and horse perform a series of movements, lead, gait and pace changes, and circles with

Thoroughbred Park. downtown Lexington, Kentucky. *Photograph by author.*

the barest evident movement on the part of the rider. This shows the ability of the rider to command his or her horse. The second (and sometimes a third) day is a timed run over miles of pasture, jumps, streams, roads and tracks to show the stamina of horse and rider fit for battle. Finally, the last day is stadium jumping inside an area, with a series of jumps to demonstrate that even after a "battle," horse and rider are able to perform. One of the world's premier Three Day Events is the Land Rover, formerly the Rolex, at the Kentucky Horse Park in Lexington, Kentucky.[18]

Owning, training and racing horses, and training riders beyond military and farm use began when English knights returned from the Crusades with fast Arab horses in the twelfth century.[19] During the reign of King Richard (1189–99), the first recorded purse was offered for a race of three miles. The horses were ridden by knights. Successor kings had large stud farms for breeding and held race meets. Charles I owned 139 stallions.[20]

The return of the Stuarts to the throne in 1660 with Charles II marked what is generally considered the beginnings of the modern era of horse racing. He was the first king to race horses under his own name.[21] Finally, during Queen Anne's time (1702–14), the practice of two-horse match races

Red Mile Racecourse. *Photograph by author.*

gave way to a field of several horses and public wagering. Racecourses were established around England, each offering large purses to attract the fastest horses. Enough money was in play that it became possible to own, breed and race horses as a business. In 1750, the English Jockey Club was organized at Newmarket to make the rules and regulate English racing.[22] Finally, the English Stud Book was started in 1791 to keep track of the breeding ancestry and progeny of thoroughbreds.[23] After a few years, it was updated annually. According to the *Encyclopedia Britannica*, all thoroughbreds are the progeny of three Arabian stallions—*Darley Arabian*, *Godolphin Barb* and the *Byerly Turk*— bred to forty-three "royal mares" imported by Charles II.[24]

In contrast to the long English history of thoroughbred racing, trotting or harness racing is said to have originated in North America. The *New York Times* in an 1897 article attributed it to early Dutch settlers. Anyone with a two-wheeled cart and a horse could race. By 1879, the term "standardbred"[25] had come to apply to this breed, and a parallel system of racetracks was developed for harness racing, including the famous Red Mile in Lexington, Kentucky, named for the red clay in its track surface.[26]

RACING IN EARLY AMERICA

One observer commented that gambling is as American as apple pie and older than the *Mayflower*.[27] Certainly that applied to horse racing.

Just four years after Charles II ascended to the throne, the commander of the British troops occupying New Amsterdam (present-day New York City) laid out a two-mile racetrack on Long Island called Newmarket, after the famous track in England. Colonel Richard Nicolls oversaw organized racing and offered a silver cup to the winner.[28]

King Charles II was very attracted to horses, women and gambling, and his colonial governors in America followed his lead in favoring racing.[29] The Long Island track is put forth as the birthplace of racing in this country. The residents of New York City eventually built a track in lower Manhattan to bring racing closer to home. In more wooded areas, where clearing land for a mile oval was more difficult, quarter-mile races down roads and streets became popular. The practice brought the obvious dangers, and communities started trying to ban racing in the public streets. As early as 1674, Plymouth, Massachusetts, passed an ordinance forbidding racing in the town streets. About a century later, Connecticut enacted a state law setting the penalty for racing in the streets as the forfeit of the rider's horse and a forty-shilling fine.[30]

Rhode Island claims to be the birthplace of the horse-breeding industry, based on the fact that early in colonial times a large tract of land on the west side of Narragansett Bay was set aside and fenced off for a breeding operation. At one time, as many as one thousand horses were on Rhode Island farms, and their offspring were shipped to southern colonies and even the Caribbean. A one-mile track was established at Sandy Neck Beach in South Kingston.[31]

Another contender for the crown of birthplace, however, is Virginia, based on the fact that most of the ports through which valuable breeding stock was imported from England were Virginian.[32] By the late seventeenth century, horse races were regular events in Virginia, primarily on quarter-mile sprints.[33] In contrast to the multi-mile races at oval tracks, where a horse's endurance was a major factor, quarter-mile racing put a premium on speed. Beyond the breeding of what became known as the quarter horse, with physical traits better for sprinting, there were two other developments. First, for speed to be relevant beyond just the first horse to cross the finish line but useful in comparing horses (and selecting for breeding), the distance run had to be the same. This led to standardization of race distances. The second change was that, instead of waiting until a horse was more developed and older (racing at four years old), owners started racing horses a year or even two earlier. The first formal racetrack in Virginia was established at 1752 on the Westover plantation in Gloucester. This was the site of the first thoroughbred race in America. Some claim that horse races were in Henrico County in 1674.[34]

By the middle of the seventeenth century, horse races were common events, usually conducted on Saturday afternoons on a straight track course marked off with stakes where the judges stood.[35] These were viewed as great events, and the crowds watching seem to have been large. In addition to the gentry competing in the race, regular farmers and planters, town residents and even servants came out to the races. Of course, large crowds attract vendors, and there was frequently a "brisk trade" in cider and brandy.[36]

In addition to the quarter horse, another uniquely American breed was the Narragansett Pacer, so called for having been bred in that area of Rhode Island. They were bred in great numbers in the 1700s. Paul Revere is said to have ridden a Narragansett Pacer on his famous ride. George Washington owned and raced a Pacer in 1768. Its origins are unknown but probably evolved from interbreeding between English and Dutch horses that arrived in New England in the early 1600s with the first colonists. The Pacers were great to ride, with a comfortable gait and long on endurance. Their sure-footedness made them stable rides over rough colonial paths and early roads. As roads improved and more people drove in carts and wagons, the Pacer lost popularity. It is reported that the last of the breed died in 1880.[37]

The thoroughbred breed was developed in England in the late 1600s and early 1700s and is defined as being able to trace ancestry back to the "Royal Mares" imported under James I and Charles I or to one of three Arabian stallions also imported in this era.[38] By the mid-1700s in the colonies, second- and third-generation Virginia planters had been able to accumulate large plantations and desired to emulate the lifestyle of the English gentry. As a consequence, they began to import quantities of Arabian and thoroughbred stock.[39] The first Arabian blood came to Virginia as early as 1732. One student of Virginia racing history has identified the names and pedigrees of fifty thoroughbred stallions and thirty mares imported to that state by 1774. All of them were descendants of the three Arabian stallions. Thoroughbreds are not built for sprinting but for running over longer distances. Racing, particularly in the South, began to adopt the mile oval track format, run over the mile in three or four heats. A horse that finished more than an eighth of a mile behind the winner in a particular heat was eliminated from the next heat.[40] This, of course, led to the need for the familiar distance marking posts along a track.

Race associations and jockey clubs were formed to establish rules for racing. The 1830 Kentucky Association in Lexington, for example, had thirty-six "Rules and Regulations" that established racing dates, officers and judges and their duties and authority to settle disputes and determine winners, eligibility to enter a horse (only an association member), jockey uniforms, the weights particular horses were to carry based on age, how wagers were to be made and the effect thereon if a horse is distanced and does not run in the next heat.[41] One rule enforced early in American racing was that only "gentlemen" could enter horses to race. In York County, Virginia, in 1674, a local tailor wagered two thousand pounds of tobacco that his horse could beat another. The local court fined him one hundred pounds of tobacco on the grounds that it was "contrary to Law for a Labourer to make a race being a Sport only for Gentlemen."[42]

Wagers were considered to be legal agreements and were frequently written down (along with any variation of the rules, such as giving an inferior horse a head start) or were stated before an impartial third party. The Virginia courts treated "race covenants" as binding contracts. If one party did not fulfill his side of the agreement, the other could bring suit in the county court. The first matter before the court would be to determine if the parties had properly made written or verbal record of the agreement. One case was dismissed because there was no proof that "money was stacked down nor Contract in writing made one of which in such cases is by law required." For these reasons, there were a number of people involved in conducting a race, not just a starter and finish judges but someone to hold the stakes and others as witnesses in the event of litigation.[43]

The legal procedure for pursuing a claim arising out of a race was detailed and ensured due process. If a party deemed himself cheated or otherwise damaged in a wager, he gathered his witnesses and brought suit in the county court. The court comprised a group of justices of the peace. If they agreed there was good cause to sue, the matter was then put before a jury of twelve freeholders to determine whether an agreement had been violated or a race run fairly. If there was enough money involved to warrant it, an appeal could be taken to the Virginia general court, which comprised the governor and his council. Surviving records indicate that the courts took enforcement of a racing dispute on the same level of seriousness as a criminal matter or probation of a will.[44]

Although not strictly of the colonial period, mention should be made of the equine interests of our early politicians. Founding Fathers such as Washington, Jefferson, Madison, Jackson and Monroe were all "turf men."[45] George Washington helped to organize races in Alexandria and belonged to its jockey club as well as the Maryland Jockey Club. He kept a register of his winnings and losses as he attended races in the region.[46] The biggest race in Virginia at the time was called the Subscription Plate, run at Williamsburg. Washington regularly contributed toward the purse. Jefferson was regarded as a "master horse breeder" with one of the finest stables in Virginia.[47] Washington and Jefferson both worked to improve the breeds of not only thoroughbreds but also saddle, work and carriage horses. Andrew Jackson was such a fan and participant that he kept a racing stable at the White House while he was president and raced his horses under his nephew's name—a practice described as an "open secret" in Washington and probably a technical violation of the club rules and regulations. Ulysses S. Grant was the last active horseman of our presidents. He bred trotters and enjoyed taking a sulky and driving at high speed down Pennsylvania Avenue.[48]

In sum, horse racing was the primary organized sport in colonial America and, similar to the sports rivalries between modern communities on the basketball court, town rivalry often centered on which could claim the best horses.[49]

THE CHURCH HORSES BUILT

O r, perhaps more accurately, it is the church built almost entirely with significant monetary contributions from horsemen and the horse industry across the country.[50]

The church is the Church of the Good Shepherd, an Episcopal congregation in Lexington, Kentucky.

The year was 1923. Various state legislatures across the country had been outlawing pari-mutuel wagering on horse racing as a means to drive tracks out of business and thus end the evil of gambling.[51] A bill to do the same in Kentucky was being debated in the legislature and, of course, in public meetings across the state.

The church began as a mission outreach of Christ Church Episcopal in downtown Lexington, first on South Broadway in 1888, then at a larger frame church on Maxwell. However, in 1918, a fire destroyed the structure. A new lot was purchased at the entrance to Bell Court, and work began on building a parish house.[52]

About this time, the Reverend Thomas Lever Settle, an Englishman who had come to Lexington after World War I, was appointed to Good Shepherd. While the parish house was dedicated on February 1, 1921, there were as yet no plans or funds to build a sanctuary. Even without that, at the request of the congregation, the status of the small church was changed from a mission to an independent congregation.

Enter the world of politics and the movement to outlaw pari-mutual wagering. As discussed in another chapter, pari-mutual wagering machines,

Church of the Good Shepherd. *Photograph by author.*

a kind of primitive early computer or calculating machine, had replaced the systems of on-track bookmakers that had dominated betting in the United States for several decades. A track relied for its income on a percentage of the amount of money wagered. Bookmaking had been prohibited when the Kentucky state racing commission adopted pari-mutuel wagering. If that were now banned, the tracks would have no source of income and would have to close, as in fact had been the case in other states. The number of working tracks had fallen from 314 in 1897 to a mere 23 by 1910.[53] At least four of the remaining tracks were in Kentucky, two of those in Lexington.

A large crowd assembled in the courtroom of the county courthouse to hear speakers on each side of the issue. The only minister to speak was Reverend Settle. He told the people that he knew firsthand the evils of bookmaking, having experienced bookies in England before entering the ministry. "With the bookmaker, the crooked owner can bet that his horse will lose," he said, "You can't do that with the pari-mutuels." He continued: "Before I went into the ministry, being an Englishman, I used to go occasionally to the races, and also being an Englishman, I occasionally bet on them. The greatest fun I found in doing it was catching the bookmaker out of line. You can't do that with the pari-mutuel." Reverend Settle was given a standing ovation by the crowd, which included many horsemen. He was asked to repeat his speech to the Kentucky General Assembly, which he did. The measure was ultimately defeated by only one vote.

The grateful horsemen offered $50,000 and a new car, which he declined. They continued to seek some way to express their thanks, and Settle decided to ask for funds for a new church. The fund drive became a project of the Thoroughbred Horse Association of Kentucky, and many donations were made from the horse industry, even small donations from the stable help, whose jobs were now preserved. One person even gave a horse, which was then auctioned. Between $200,000[54] and $300,000[55] was raised to build the stone church and sanctuary, which was completed by 1926.

In the narthex, or entryway of the church, is a plaque with the following dedication:

To the glory of God this Church is given
to Him by the lovers of the horse from all
over the country as a token of appreciation
of their Father's goodness to His children-man

Jockeys' Silks

To a racing fan trackside, they are part of the dramatic color of race; to an owner, they're a trademark and symbol of the stable; to a jockey, they're a uniform; to the track announcer, they're a helpful hint of which horse is which as he calls the race; but most important, they are an aid to the track judges in distinguishing one horse from another.[56] In a photo finish, for example, only the nose of the horse away from the camera and the jockey's back and cap might be visible behind a horse nearer to the camera.

Ancient Persian, Chinese and Indian paintings and pottery demonstrate both horse racing and the use of colors for identity. Organized racing was conducted by the ancient Greeks.[57] By 624 BC, Greek riders wore colored cloaks into the arena called "chlamys."[58] However, when it was time for the race, they dropped the cloaks and rode bare as well as barebacked. Some horses may even have been dyed colors.[59]

The Romans introduced colored tunics and headbands. Emperor Nero's color was green, for example, and vendors in stalls outside the Coliseum sold colored headbands for attendees to wear in support of their horse.[60] The Huns, Mongols and Muslims all put different squads of cavalry in different colored gear.[61]

In the Middle Ages, heraldry and armored knights led to a need for identification on the battlefield; coats of arms and crests began to appear on shields and on tunics worn over the armor. Heraldry also provided the basic design elements used for silks.[62] The designs moved first to the doublets of housemen and footmen of the noble. When he started racing, it was natural to adopt the doublet for the jockey.

The first mention of individual colors was under Henry VIII in 1515. By 1762, the variety and overlap of designs led horsemen to regulate the use. At a meeting at Newmarket, England, a racing town, the Jockey Club adopted a rule that all horsemen should adopt and register their "colours." Nineteen gentlemen at the meeting registered theirs. His Royal Highness the Duke of Cumberland chose purple; His Grace the Duke of Grafton registered sky blue. "Straw" was the color chosen by the Duke of Devonshire; as of 1993, his family still sported that color. Originally, all caps were black, but by 1771, colored caps, bands and stripes appear and the material moved from velvet to satin.[63]

The practice of jockeys wearing silks, or satins, carried over to the English colonies, but not the requirement of registration. Although jockey clubs were formed locally to govern racing in various venues in the colonies (and later, states), the focus was not on silks. The Lexington (Kentucky) Jockey Club adopted a rule in 1826 that all riders were to wear silk jackets and caps, but it did not attempt a design register.[64] It was not until the New York Board of Control, which regulated races in that state, started a register in

Silks. *Bill Straus.*

1890.[65] While today the (American) Jockey Club has a master registry, state racing commissions also can set up registers, which can result in duplication. By 1893, the drivers at trotting tracks began to adopt designs that finally became standardized in the 1950s.[66]

Today, there are more than fifteen thousand designs registered in Great Britain, even though owners are limited to eighteen colors, twenty-five shapes and twelve sleeves. In the United States, there is a broader choice of colors and designs, including original ones, but each must be approved by the club.[67]

Unusual or unique designs include a former NBA referee's black and white stripes that resemble his on-court uniform, a New York Knicks fan whose silks have a basketball on the back, and a composer whose design is musical notes inside a circle. One set of owners who frequent a pub at Saratoga have silks with a dartboard, violin and pint of stout. Queen Elizabeth II's silks are purple and scarlet, with gold embroidery and a black velvet cap. They date back to King George IV in the 1820s.[68] Her black cap also has fringe, which is permitted only to royalty.[69]

THEY'RE OFF!

T he crashing of gates flung open, the ringing of the starter's bell and
the unleashed fury of a cavalry charge of horses is how we experience
the start of a thoroughbred race. At a harness track, an automobile
with track-spanning gates hinged to the rear bumpers brings the trotters and
their sulkies from a standing start slowly up to speed before the gates are
swung forward and the auto speeds away to give the drivers an open track.
At the Red Mile in Lexington, the automobile is a 1995 Cadillac Fleetwood,
the rear seats modified, raised and reversed so the starter can look backward
to watch the horses and sulkies. The gate is sixty feet wide.[70]

It wasn't always so easy to get a fair start.

When a race was a match race between two horses over a long distance, it
was not difficult to start; but as the field of horses in a race increased and the
distance shortened, it became much more difficult.[71] Although the dictionary
does not relate the origins of the noun *jockey*, meaning the rider, and the verb
jockey, meaning to move around to attempt to get a better position, it appears
the two meanings came into use about the same time, as riders would jockey
for an advantage at the start. Starting methods varied. One starter is quoted
as saying, "I shall require you all to draw up about forty or fifty yards behind
the post, walk gently up to it, and when I remove my hat from my head and
say 'Go' it will be a start."[72]

Other starts at times were effected by holding a rope across the track;
the race started when it dropped. An advertisement in a New York City
newspaper in 1781 pleaded for the return of "seventy yards" of new white

rope to be used at the races, offering a twenty-guinea reward.[73] Other methods included the dropping or waving of a flag. One writer described it as the "fine old art of the man with the red flag, facing a crowd of 10,000 people with 15 or so thoroughbreds to line up."[74] Robes, ribbons and even wooden barriers were tried.[75]

By the later years of the nineteenth century, inventors were coming up with mechanical alternatives. An early version involved a large heavy strip of rubber held by the starter on one end and an assistant on the other. This ultimately was discarded as the riders discovered it was nothing more than a huge rubber band that they could move into and stretch into an advanced starting position.[76]

The most successful was the "Gray Gate," designed by Reuben G. Gray of Sydney, Australia. It consisted of six strands of dark-brown heavy rope strung on a frame that stretched across the track. The frame in turn was rigged onto poles set in concrete with pulleys, weights and ropes. Initially set at four and a half feet off the ground to the bottom rope, when released, it sprang up to a height of twelve feet, clearing the way for the horses to start. It even had the innovation of having small tags with numbers on the top rope to indicate where a numbered horse should line up. It became the standard starting machine around the world in the early decades of the twentieth century.[77]

Jockeys were not pleased with the new machines. Not only did they reduce their ability to "jockey" for position at the start, but the machines also affected them personally. Jockeys were fined for infractions on the track, mostly at the start; but the number of infractions at the start radically decreased. Latonia collected $800 in 1895, but only $50 the next year when a gate was installed. These monies went into a fund to help injured jockeys so the size of the fund diminished.[78]

Hoyt Clay Puett was credited by the *Lexington Herald Leader* in 1973 with being the inventor of an electronic starting gate, replacing manual operations.[79] His gates had slots for each horse, metal front gates and padded rear panels. The electric latch was modeled on bomb-release mechanisms in military aircraft, and the locks were released by pulling a trigger.[80]

However, following a similar story in the *Daily Racing Form* in 1994 crediting Puett, a descendant of Marshall Cassidy asserted that Cassidy had invented the modern gate with front doors on individual slots, webbing at the back, overhead partitions and steerable wheels for moving at a track in Mexico in 1930, crediting Puett only with taking those innovations and starting a successful gate construction firm.[81]

Starting gate. *Bill Straus.*

Along the way, metal extensions were tried, about four feet long and welded to the doors of the gate with a series of seventeen rubber rollers. Intended to guide the horses as they started, in fact, they caused an increase in injuries at the start; this model was discontinued.[82]

Today, there are two kinds of gates, the United Gate with flat front doors and the Pruett Gate with V-shaped doors.[83] Both are locked closed by strong electromagnets. When the starter presses the button, the current is released and powerful springs yank open the gate doors.

Resting in Peace

What do you do when a famous horse dies? In Kentucky, you place it to rest in an equine cemetery. Thoroughbred Heritage lists almost 170 equine cemeteries in the commonwealth.[84]

The first Kentucky horse to have a grave marker was the thoroughbred *Lexington*. At his death in 1875, he was standing at stud at Woodburn Farm in Woodford County.[85] Then owner Robert A. Alexander erected a marble stone to mark the grave. Others then followed the practice.[86]

Lexington was originally named *Darley* by Dr. Elisha Warfield at his farm The Meadows in Lexington when foaled in 1850. He was not raced until he was three, and then he bolted at the start and ran two miles before being brought back to the start. Even then, he led the field in each of two heats. This brought *Lexington* to the attention of Richard Ten Broeck, one of the owners of the Metairie Race Course in New Orleans, who bought the horse for $5,000 and renamed him.[87] He won six of seven races and was second in the other, and he set the record time for four miles. When he started to go blind at age five, he was retired to stud at Nantura Stud in Midway, Kentucky, before being purchased two years later by Alexander.[88]

A few months after his burial, his body was exhumed and his skeleton came to be displayed in the Smithsonian in Washington, D.C. Finally, in 2010, his skeleton was returned home to Kentucky and is displayed at the International Museum of the Horse at the Kentucky Horse Park outside Lexington.[89]

Above: Hamburg Place Equine Cemetery. *Left*: Grave marker for *Merrick*. *Photographs by author*.

Why all this attention for a horse who ran in only seven races? He led the sire list for sixteen years, two of them after his death.[90] The sire list tracks the annual combined winnings of a stud's offspring. This is a record that still stands. He sired at least 600 foals.[91] Of these, 238 were winners; of them, 84 were graded stakes winners. Had not racing been interrupted in many places during the Civil War and many of his offspring used in cavalry units on both sides, these numbers would be greater.[92]

According to Thoroughbred Heritage, there are at least 165 equine cemeteries and graves in Kentucky.

One of the largest is on famous Calumet Farm outside Lexington, where, as of 2014, there were 63 gravestones. The stallion *Bull Lea*'s

Hamburg Place equine graveyard. *Photograph by author.*

monument is centered in the tree-lined area. His seven winning colts are buried and marked in a semicircle in front of him. In another semicircle are his daughters, who produced Kentucky Derby winners. Other grave markers are to the left and right.[93]

Another famous equine cemetery, one easily accessed, as it is adjacent to a public street, is the Hamburg Place Cemetery. It is one of the oldest dedicated to horses. John E. Madden developed Hamburg Place farm starting with 235 acres he purchased in 1897 with the proceeds from selling the racehorse *Hamburg*, growing eventually to 2,300 contiguous acres.[94] In all, eighteen horses are buried there.[95] Beginning in 2005, the farm has since been developed commercially into a regional shopping center as well as residential, commercial and office areas. The streets in the development are all named after Hamburg Place horses; the relocated cemetery is on Sir Barton Way.

Another equine cemetery made the local news in 2017 when the owner of the farm, who knew of its equine cemetery, discovered an overgrown cemetery with graves tracing to Lexington's earliest days. The horses buried there include the 1959 Kentucky Derby winner *Tommy Lee*.[96]

McDowell Speedway

Before there were four-wheeled vehicles powered by engines racing around NASCAR speedways, there were four-wheeled carriages in races called speedways pulled by horses. Carriage races were not popular in the pioneer era in Kentucky for the lack of good roads; with the advent of large oval racetracks with level surfaces and paved roads, they became more frequent.

By the turn of the twentieth century, there was the League of Amateur Driving Clubs, with local clubs in many cities, including Boston, New York City, Syracuse, Pittsburgh, Chicago, Detroit, Memphis and Lexington.[97]

As early as 1872, match races were held on Lexington's tracks. The *Daily Press* reported on a spirited four-heat race among five local men. The race had been moved for an unstated reason from the trotting track[98] to Dr. Herr's track.[99] The unacknowledged reporter set the scene: "[Q]uite a respectable company assembled at the latter place about 3½ o'clock, and collecting in groups under the shady trees smoked cigars, ruminated, chewing the cud of sweet and bitter fine cut,[100] and talked horse in a way that would have mystified any one but a thoroughbred Kentuckian."

This was a "gentleman's race," with no betting permitted or betting pools sold. The five "reinsmen" were James C. Thompson driving a seven-year-old gelding, R.W. Preston with his four-year-old filly, Allie Hunt driving *Cricket*, A.J. Reed driving a brown gelding, and one Carrol—evidently well known, as his first name was not given—behind a four-year-old bay mare.

Timers, judges and a starter were selected, and the drivers drew lots for position. The first three lined up across and the last behind them. After the first heat was run, the horses were cooled off briefly, and they lined up for the second race. "The horses came thundering down the homestretch, rolling the dust in clouds from their heels. This time the winners of the first heat came in third and fourth. For the third heat the three slowest horses were allowed to start in front and tried to preserve a chance of winning by staying abreast and not allowing the faster horses through. However, one broke for the wire and the opening allowed a faster carriage to speed through and win." The reporter, having breathlessly reported the race, concluded: "So ended the sport, and the drivers, having dusted themselves and donned their coats, came to town in good humor with themselves and each other. No bones were broken and no money was lost on the race. For mere roadsters, and driven, too, to heavy buggies, the time made was excellent, and no one has cause to be dissatisfied with his horse."[101]

The 1904 summer Horse Show and Matinee Race meeting included "two speedway rings." The events were only open to members of the Driving Club, and a total of sixteen silver julip cups were awarded. Curiously, the local Elks Club also arranged a mule race, described as a mile steeplechase race with objects and obstacles of various kinds being placed on the track "which the mules must jump, run over or balk at." The Elks drum corps in red caps and coats and white trousers performed, and at the end there was a pony race for boys under fifteen years old.[102]

The Elks fair for 1902 included not only roadster (carriage) and harness horse races, but also saddlehorse and thoroughbred events, beef and dairy cattle, ponies and mules. Floral decoration prizes were also given for the best decorated two-horse, run about or road and pony carts.[103]

At this time, another significant trend was underway that would lead to a most unusual speedway. For decades, under state law, while a city maintained its streets, roads outside the city limits had been licensed or franchised to private toll road companies. In the later part of the nineteenth century, there was a movement to authorize the private companies to sell their interests to the government. This was encouraged by masked attacks on toll buildings and their operators—in Kentucky, these were called the "toll road wars." Tollhouses were burned and toll keepers whipped.[104] On July 23, 1897, the Fayette County Fiscal Court (the governing body) met to discuss buying three roads, the Richmond, Georgetown and Nicholasville pikes, with the goal of making travel free of tolls.[105] The militant and unlawful attacks, of course, had the effect of reducing the prices of the rights-of-way. While the acquisition of the other roads was comparatively uneventful, Richmond Road's acquisition took an interesting turn.

Carriages before a race. Lexington Herald, *1906*.

Henry Clay's Ashland farm was divided among heirs and some tracts retained by children and some sold. The main tract with his house became the property of Transylvania University and the site of its new college, Kentucky A&M (which eventually separated and became the University of Kentucky). By 1878, the two schools decided to split. The State of Kentucky took possession of Ashland and, giving the college a two-year lease, put it up for sale. The college took the offer of the city to move to the core of its present site.[106] In 1882, Major Henry Clay McDowell and his wife, Ann Clay, daughter of Henry Clay Jr., purchased the 324-acre estate with an eye to restoring it, both house and grounds, after the hard use by the college.

The McDowells made many improvements to the estate, restored the equine breeding operation, built stables and made other improvements. A visitor in 1898 observed that "Ashland is probably in better condition today than when Henry Clay worked and planned, and superintended its fair acres." Major McDowell also developed a "first-class" standardbred breeding farm.[107] Standardbreds are used for carriage racing.

McDowell served in the Union army during the Civil War, rising to the rank of major. He had many business interests and was president of the

Lexington and Eastern Railway. In 1883, he purchased *Dictator*, one of four major sons of standardbred champion *Hambletonian* and a major sire in his own right.

Across Richmond Road, which was in the process of being purchased by the county, lay the even larger estate of the Preston family, likely the family of the reinsman noted earlier. William Preston was one of the early investors in the new privately owned Lexington water company. A tract of his land on the south side of the road just past the Clay family property would become the lake for water service to Lexington.

The Lexington Hydraulic & Manufacturing Company was formed and began construction of a lake in a deep valley through which flowed the West Hickman Creek, erecting a dam along Mount Tabor Pike to the east. Over ten years, the reservoir's system was expanded to more than two hundred acres. The company developed one shore of the lake into a public park and stocked the lake with fish. In the fall of 1897, it opened a new clubhouse on the property with an attached boathouse that extended one hundred feet into the lake. The second floor contained a locker room and beds for overnight stays by guests. The Lake Ellerslie Fishing Club was headquartered there.

In August 1897, McDowell purchased a fifty-foot-wide strip of land from Preston, running from the city limits two miles out along and beside Richmond Road to the lake. He then deeded the land to the county under the conditions that it construct an improved dirt road level with the road, that no streetcar or railroad was to be put in it and that the county would repair or replace farm fences taken down in the process. By the following spring, the newly improved way became a "pleasure drive" for carriages and trotting horses out to the lake. Carriage races with matched teams of horses would be held along this speedway, with crowds gathering to watch the finish. A Chicago newspaper called it "one of the best drives of its kind in the country." The county contracted for it to be harrowed and worked in the summer "until it is almost as fast as a regulation track."

The Elks Club hosted carriage races each year at the Kentucky Trotting Horse Association track (today's Red Mile), and it openly encouraged the use of the speedway for training horses and for pleasure road driving. Many townspeople utilized it to go to the lake for events and picnics. No doubt it afforded McDowell great pleasure to drive his carriage, perhaps in local competition with Preston and others, out of his front gate and around his speedway.

McDowell was hardly alone in his sport. Wealthy men like New Yorkers Jerome Leonard and Billy Klair (founder of Belmont racecourse) were skilled

Left: McDowell Speedway/Richmond Road. The speedway was out on the right and back on the left. *Right*: H.C. McDowell monument. *Photographs by author.*

coachmen who would drive their own four-horse heavy carriages, filled with guests, servants and food and drink to the track.[108]

McDowell died in 1899. The following spring, H.H. Gratz, heir of Benjamin Gratz, for whom Gratz Park is named,[109] appeared before the County Fiscal Court to request that the boulevard be known as the H.C. McDowell Speedway and a monument erected recognizing McDowell's key role in the roadway improvements.[110] The request was approved and the monument shown in the accompanying photographs erected, although between residential developments and road widenings the exact location has moved a couple of times.

With the advent of automobiles, carriage racing and equine use of the McDowell Speedway lessened. In the early decades of the twentieth century, both the McDowell and Preston farms were subject to residential subdivision, although the deeds to the Preston lands described them as fronting on the McDowell Boulevard. In 1911, the county paved Richmond Road with asphalt to the lake. The McDowell family resisted changes to the speedway, but in 1914, an agreement was reach with all property owners and the county for both the road and the speedway to be paved as a divided highway, the old road being one way out of town and the former speedway

Carriage Racing at the World Equestrian Games 2017, Kentucky Horse Park. *David Stephenson.*

being one way in. Two years later, the roadways were widened to two lanes each and, eventually, crossing cuts were made in the parkway in between for residents, leaving new streets to cross over, a feature not needed when only large horse farms lined the way. The parkway was improved in 1914 with rows of trees.

In time, the memory of the McDowell Speedway dimmed, leaving only the monument as a reminder. Today's automobile driver heading along Richmond Road for downtown Lexington has no notion that he is motoring down the speedway's track.

As a final note, the first speeding ticket in Fayette County was issued on November 1, 1904, to one Alex G. Morgan for driving his automobile at an excessive speed down the McDowell Speedway.[111]

America's First Professional Athlete Class

Few know that the first professional athletes—as a group, not particular individuals—were African American jockeys.[112] Most learned to ride under African American trainers or other jockeys literally in the farm system of the southern states, riding their owners' mounts on tracks across the South—but only in the South; putting a skilled slave on a fast horse in a free state was not considered a good plan. The customary job route was that a likely young farmworker would be assigned to the stables. When talent was shown, a former jockey turned trainer would teach the boy to ride. When he became too old, or too heavy, to continue riding, he could become a trainer and complete the cycle.[113]

After emancipation, however, these highly skilled jockeys were free to ride for whomever and wherever they could. A large number migrated to northern tracks. Oliver Lewis and others are described in *Race Horse Men* as being "everywhere" in the 1880s. In any event, the southern tracks, horse farms and breeding stock were decimated by the Civil War, which was almost completely fought over that land. The region experienced a 49 percent decline in wealth, and racing shifted to the North and to families with wealth who desired to display it.[114]

Thoroughbred racing has been described as America's first and only truly national sport, predating baseball, football, basketball and all others. The *Spirit of the Times* reported that by the 1880s, African American jockeys "have almost monopolized the best mounts, and have been singularly successful."[115]

One famous African American trainer was Edward "Brown Dick" Brown, born a slave in 1850 in Fayette County outside Lexington. Robert A. Alexander bought him in 1857. Brown first rode for Alexander's Woodburn Farm, then he trained. As a slave, Brown rode the famous *Asteroid*.[116] After he was freed, he remained at the farm. As a jockey, he won the Belmont aboard *Kingfisher*, who was trained by another famous African American, Raleigh Colson.[117] After Alexander's death, he trained for Daniel Swigert, nephew[118] and former Woodburn farm manager, and trained the 1877 Kentucky Derby winner *Baden-Baden*.[119] Brown would later be elected into racing's hall of fame.

What follows are profiles of six famous African American jockeys.

OLIVER LEWIS

Oliver Lewis won the first Kentucky Derby in 1875 on *Aristides*. Of the fifteen horses in the race, all but two were carrying black jockeys. *Aristides* was part of a two-horse entry by owner Hal Price McGrath, whose strategy was for Lewis to ride out to an early and fast lead to tire the competing horses, then pull back to allow his favored horse, *Chesapeake*, to win. *Aristides*, however, did not comply with Lewis's efforts to restrain him, and *Chesapeake* was in the middle of the pack. McGrath waved to Lewis to go for the win, and he did in the fastest time for a three-year-old horse carrying only one hundred pounds. The other horse finished eighth. A $105 ticket in the auction pools[120] paid $495, McGrath won the $2,850 purse and a sterling silver punch bowl valued at $1,000.

Oliver Lewis. *Portrait by Adelin Wichman, photograph by Andy Mead.*

Lewis and *Aristides* nearly won the Belmont Stakes the next month, but McGrath was following his same strategy and ordered Lewis to defer to another McGrath horse. He did, and McGrath collected some $30,000 in bets. Lewis reportedly quit riding at some point and became a bookmaker.[121] Lexington would name a new street Oliver Lewis Way in time.

ISAAC MURPHY

Murphy's year of birth is disputed, varying from 1856 to 1864. Mooney asserts he was born a slave, while Edward Hotaling says he was the freeborn son of a Union soldier who was at Camp Nelson on the Kentucky River, having enlisted in 1864. He was named Isaac Burns, but upon his father's death in the 1860s, his mother moved back into her father's house with Isaac and his sister. His grandfather was Green Murphy, and young Isaac took his last name as his own.[122]

Isaac Murphy. Portrait by Adelin Wichman, photograph by Andy Mead.

After starting work on a horse farm as an exercise boy, Murphy went to work for noted black trainer Eli Jorden at age twelve. Two years later, he rode in his first race in Louisville just five days after Lewis won the first Kentucky Derby.[123] He finished last. The following year, he won at Lexington, and his career was taking off. In 1877, he won in his debut at Saratoga and continued that year to win the St. Ledger at Louisville, the Breckinridge Stakes at Pimlico and other races. In 1879, he was second in the Kentucky Derby.

In that same year, Murphy engineered a come-from-behind win over two more favored horses in the Travers at Saratoga. After the race, he was interviewed by a writer for the *Spirit of the Times*, a national racing publication. Hotaling details the interview over several pages where Murphy describes the strategy he used to slip up on the other jockeys in the race to judge their mounts' stamina without making them think he was a threat. The race was for a mile and three quarters, and his winning time was just over three minutes. But, as Hotaling described it, "[h]e turned moments into something almost like leisure, racing up, dropping back, feeling out the competition, adapting tactics, and keeping a sharp eye on his colt."[124] The writer concluded that Murphy was "one of the best jockeys in America." His record that year to the date of the interview showed it: thirty-five races, twenty-two wins and one tie.[125]

The 1880s witnessed a boom in the horse-racing world as new money made in mining out West made wealthy men who entered into the field. Murphy was riding for many wealthy men and their stables and was able to dictate the terms of his riding contracts.[126] He married in 1882 and bought a small house on Megowan Street in Lexington. The next year, they bought what some described as a mansion on Third Street. It had ten rooms with a rooftop observatory from which Murphy could watch, and scout, his human and equine competition running at the nearby Kentucky Association track. Murphy had his own carriage and a white valet. He and his wife did not sell their first house but kept it as rental property.[127]

By the late 1880s, Murphy was "the leading light of a whole cadre of black contemporaries."[128] With annual earnings of $12,000 in 1887, Murphy was, according to Hotaling, America's highest-paid athlete.[129] At one time, he was paid $10,000 a year by one owner just to be "on call."[130] In 1890, he won the Suburban in New York on *Salvator*, beating a rival named *Tenny*. The defeated horse owner demanded a rematch, which was scheduled for Coney Island in June. Murphy won by a head. The next month, the rivalry continued at new Monmouth Park in New Jersey. It was another win for Murphy. Two weeks later, a large party was held to celebrate the victories, attended by Murphy and the white elites. He was at the top.

The fall came two days after the party, when he appeared drunk and barely able to stay in the saddle in a race, coming in last and even falling off his horse before the finish. People in the crowd rushed the track to catch his horse and put him back on to trot to the finish. Friends carried him to the jockeys' locker room and hurried him away.[131]

Controversy followed Murphy from that day on. Theories flew that he had been drunk, or that he had been starving himself so much to keep his weight down that he had not fully recovered from the party. Murphy always maintained that he had been poisoned and was never well since.[132]

The following January, however, and probably back up to his "winter weight," he and his wife gave a large party at their Lexington house. Attendees included Oliver Lewis. That May, Murphy won his third Kentucky Derby.[133] He won a respectable thirty-two races that year; but he only won six times in forty-two races the next year. Rides on quality horses were decreasing.

Starting in 1893, Murphy bought some two-year-old horses and tried his hand at training but was not successful.[134] He still raced, but the question of his drinking followed him. He readily admitted that, if he won, "it was all right," but if he lost or had a poor mount, it was due to drinking.

On February 12, 1896, he died of pneumonia at his home in Lexington.[135] His lifetime record was 628 wins in 1,412 races, a 44 percent win record that still stands.[136] When the National Museum of Racing and Hall of Fame was established in 1955, Murphy was the first jockey inducted.[137]

JAMES WINKFIELD

Jimmy Winkfield was born in a small community east of Lexington in 1892, and by the time he was fourteen, he was hired to work horses at Latonia. The next year, another horseman, Bub May, hired him as a jockey. In contrast to Murphy's $10,000-a-year retainer, Winkfield was paid $10 per month plus board. Winkfield improved with each race and won forty races at an Indiana track. May gave him a three-year contract with an increase in pay to $25 per month and sent him to race in New Orleans. He raced third in the 1900 Kentucky Derby, and in 1901, May sold his contract to Patrick Dunne. Winkfield's star continued to rise as he won 161 races and was first in the Derby.[138]

Racial tensions were also rising in the racing world, and Winkfield was involved in what was called a "race war" at the Chicago track, where white jockeys, jealous of the successes of Winkfield and other blacks, initiated some incidents on and off the track. The black jockeys pushed back, and track officials had to intervene.[139]

For the 1902 Derby, Thomas Clay McDowell, a Henry Clay descendant, hired him to ride *Alan-a-Dale*, which he did for the second back-to-back Derby win since Isaac Murphy (1890 and 1891). McDowell gave him a $1,000 bonus. The following year, he finished second in the Derby. He never rode in the Kentucky Derby again and stands as the only African American to win the Derby in the twentieth century.[140]

An event in the 1903 Futurity at Sheepshead Bay was life changing. Lexington's John E. Madden asked Winkfield to ride for him, and Winkfield agreed. Then Bud May offered him $3,000 to ride for May. Winkfield switched, which infuriated Madden. Madden's horse was third, while Winkfield finished sixth. Madden told Winkfield that if he wouldn't ride for him, Madden would see to it he rode for no one. Madden had the influence to enforce his statement, and Winkfield's rides dropped by almost half the next year.[141] The next year, he left for Europe and won the Warsaw Derby, starting his European career.[142]

By 1910, Winkfield's riding in Europe and Russia was so successful that he stopped even trying to ride in the United States. His American wife sued him for abandonment and divorce, which he did not contest. He started riding for the owner of the largest stable in Poland, an Armenian oil baron. By 1917, he was the leading jockey for Czar Nicholas II and lived in a luxurious apartment across from the Kremlin with a Russian wife and a white valet. He had won the Warsaw Derby twice, the Russian Derby four times and the Emperor's Purse. In fact, he won all three of Russia's derbies—Moscow, Warsaw and St. Petersburg—a sort of czarist triple crown.[143]

The Russian Revolution arrived in 1917, however, and the Bolsheviks took a dim view of what Mooney called "a man who made an opulent living piloting the playthings of the rich." He, his wife and three children and stable hands walked 262 of the finest horses in Europe to safety in Poland (a journey of 1,100 miles) with a loss of only 10 horses.[144]

Winkfield continued on to France, where he returned to riding and winning, including the Prix du Président de la République, the Grand Prix de Deauville and other major races.[145] By 1930, when he retired from riding, he owned his own stable and horse farm outside of Paris in Maisons-Laffitte.[146] He had a lifetime total of 2,300 wins. The outbreak of World War II forced the Winkfield family to retreat to the United States, but they returned to France in 1953.[147] He remained in France until his death in 1974.[148]

JAMES "SOUP" PERKINS

James Perkins.
Portrait by Adelin Wichman, photograph by Andy Mead.

James Perkins was born in Kansas City in 1880, but his family soon moved to Lexington. His father worked with trotters and eventually not only James but also three of his brothers went into the horse business. They lived very close to the Kentucky Association track, and by age ten, James was working at the stables.[149]

At that time, he started riding; by thirteen, he was earning $4,000 per year. In two more years, he doubled that figure, winning Lexington's Phoenix Stakes and following that by winning the Kentucky Derby. Within another year, he was making enough to buy his family a brick house.[150]

He gained the nickname "Soup" from other boys around the Lexington track before he began racing. He frequently walked home for lunch and, on his return, when asked what he had for lunch, he always said "soup."[151]

By 1895, Soup Perkins was the leading jockey, with 192 wins.

Unfortunately, his career took a dramatic downturn, and in 1897, he was disqualified from racing at the Northern Kentucky track. In two more years, his racing career was over. He died in 1911. In 2011, Lexington named a street for him: Soup Perkins Alley.[152]

Willie Simms

According to Hotaling, Willie Simms ran off from his home in Georgia to get into racing because he liked the colors of jockey silks. He was born in 1870 and by age twenty-one won the 1891 featured race Spinway at Saratoga. He was the fifth-leading jockey that year, rising to second the next year. This earned him a $12,000-per-year contract from wealthy businessman and horseman Pierre Lorillard.[153]

In 1893, he won the Belmont Stakes and was the number-one jockey in the country, with 182 wins. The following year was a repeat: a win at the Belmont and top jockey.[154] This led to multiple contracts, with horsemen and trainers lining up, in order, for his services. He earned about $20,000 a year as one of

Willie Simms. Portrait by Adelin Wichman, photograph by Andy Mead.

the wealthiest jockeys in America.

Simms gave racing in England a try, the first American jockey to race there; but few mounts came his way, and he returned to Morris Park after only four months and won the Kentucky Derby in 1896. This was the first year the winning horse was draped in a blanket of roses, although the nickname "Run for the Roses" would not be coined for two more decades.[155]

Over his career, Simms won the Belmont twice, the Derby twice and the Preakness once, in 1898, making him the only African American jockey to win all three Triple Crown races. He retired in 1901 with one of the best all-time win records and died in New Jersey in 1927.[156]

Alonzo "Lonnie" Clayton

Hotaling calls Lonnie Clayton no less than a boy wonder, the youngest jockey to win the Kentucky Derby when he did.[157] Born in Kansas City, Kansas, in 1876, his family and eight brothers and sisters moved to Little Rock in 1886.[158] Two years later, he ran away from home to join a brother working as a jockey in Chicago. Two years later, in 1890, he moved to New Jersey and began his riding career. By the next year, he won his first stakes, the Champaign at Morris Park. This was followed in 1892 by the Derby victory, which he won at age fifteen.

Clayton won many races during that decade, riding across the country, winning the Kentucky Oaks twice and finishing in the money three more times in the Derby.[159] He also won the Monmouth Handicap in 1893 and the Arkansas Derby in 1895, and he finished third in the 1896 Preakness. He won 144 races in 1895 alone.[160] Like other successful black jockeys, Clayton became an "employment center" and employed as many as four full-time workers.[161]

However, he, too, encountered career-ending trouble. In 1901, he was arrested for trying to fix a race. The charges were ultimately dropped, but the damage to his reputation was done.[162] At the same time, the Jim Crow era's rising racial prejudice and a trend toward favoring white jockeys meant fewer opportunities for jockeys like Clayton.[163] The 1896 U.S. Supreme Court decision in *Plessy v. Ferguson* endorsing the concept of "separate but equal" treatment furthered the trend.[164]

Clayton retired, but, unable to continue earning money as well as he had, he sold properties he had acquired and moved to California, where he worked as a hotel bellhop. He died there in 1917 from tuberculosis.

Alonzo Clayton. *Portrait by Adelin Wichman, photograph by Andy Mead.*

END OF AN ERA

Several social trends conspired to thwart black jockeys. *Plessy* inspired and approved segregation, as did a spate of Jim Crow laws in the South, a movement to restrict black athletes in many sports and the popularization of racial determination promoting the white, Anglo-Saxon race as superior.[165] Beyond those trends, however, were the activities of the Ku Klux Klan and restricted chances for advancement, which drove African Americans away from the rural settings, where a boy could become familiar with horses, and into the cities. Finally, the influx of more wealthy men into the field, who acquired larger and larger tracts of land, drove out the small black horsemen who were the traditional starting points for future jockeys.[166] The era of dominance by black jockeys ended.

In Lexington, however, they are still honored. Streets have been named for Lewis and Perkins.[167] Murphy has memorials at the Kentucky Horse Park and African Cemetery No. 2 and has a Memorial Art Garden near where his house was.[168] Lewis, Clayton, Murphy, Perkins, Simms and Winkfield and others are featured in original portraits painted by a local artist, Adalin Wichman, in an equine display encircling the atrium of the Lexington Public Library's main branch.[169]

How Good Intentions
Almost Killed Racing

The old aphorism has it that the road to hell is paved with good intentions. In the ending decades of the nineteenth century and early decades of the twentieth, two movements collided, the effect of which was to almost kill thoroughbred racing in the United States: the Progressive or Social Gospel movement in America and the Jersey Act in England.

The Progressive Era is generally considered to have begun in the 1880s and lasted through the passage of the constitutional amendment giving women the right to vote in 1920, finally ending with the repeal of Prohibition. The Social Gospel progressives in particular sought to combat what they considered to be the negative social effects of industrialization: political corruption, saloons, gambling and prostitution. They elevated the American tradition of making one's way by good, old-fashioned hard work and were appalled at the prospect that a few well-placed bets on the right horses could result in wealth.[170]

To take a view of the scope of the issue, in 1897, there were 314 thoroughbred racetracks in the United States, in addition to the standardbred tracks.[171] The issue for the social reformers was not horse racing as such, but that there was gambling—and not so much gambling at the tracks, as there was a modicum of regulation by track authorities there. At first, bookies and their touts roamed the grounds. By 1891, Churchill Downs in Louisville set up three stands and confined the bookies there on penalty of losing permission to operate at all.[172] Even the tracks, however, were not immune.

In 1894, the operators of Chicago's Washington Park closed it down because of the "degeneration of racing from a harmless and high-class sport into a species of gambling."[173]

The real problem was seen to be the offtrack betting parlors where auction pools were sold. An auction pool was a wagering system whereby each horse in a race in turn was auctioned off to the highest bidder, and when bidding ceased, the remaining horses, if any, were grouped and auctioned as the field.[174] More than one pool would be auctioned for a race if there was sufficient interest. In this manner, a bettor might spread his risk by buying different horses in different pools. The resulting pool of money, after the house took its charge, went to the holder of the winning ticket for that pool.[175] In addition to the family suffering resulting from money lost by the bettor, these establishments sold strong drink and offered other entertainment, such as billiard tables to divert customers between races. They came to be known popularly as "pool halls," and the name "pool" came to be associated with the game.

The reformers' strategy was that, if betting were outlawed, the tracks would close and so too would the pool halls.

In 1898, New Jersey passed laws banning both gambling and horse racing. Not even August Belmont could prevent New York from outlawing gambling in 1908. Tracks and bettors turned to oral betting (the laws banned betting tickets), but further legislation attacked that practice. Finally, New York beefed up its law by providing that the officers and directors of a track could be fined and put in jail if any betting was found at their track.[176] The tracks closed.

Almost every state in the country enacted similar laws, and by 1908, the number of thoroughbred tracks had fallen by 90 percent to only thirty-one. By the 1920s, only three states allowed legal betting at racetracks—one of which was Kentucky.[177]

Not that Kentucky was immune to the reformist movement. In 1908, Louisville passed an ordinance outlawing bookmakers, and Churchill Downs had to scramble to find pari-mutuel wagering machines to hold that year's Kentucky Derby.[178] Racing interests in the Kentucky House of Representatives used a parliamentary maneuver to block a vote on a proposed five-cent tax on wagers.[179] A bill to outlaw pari-mutuel wagering was before the General Assembly in 1924, and it easily passed the House but lost, 24–10, in the Senate. Racing was retained in Kentucky by all of 10 votes.[180]

The defeat was attributed in large part to the strength and political power of the Kentucky Jockey Club, discussed in more detail later. At one time, the club was alleged to have some thirty legislators on its payroll.[181] The Louisville *Courier Journal* opined that the "Kentucky Jockey Club, supported by the American Book Company, maintains a sinister but effective control of legislation in Kentucky."[182] The American Book Company was a trade association or union of bookmakers.

In 1927, betting was a key issue in the governor's race, with each candidate taking clear but opposite stands on whether to ban gambling. As James Duane Bolin describes it, it was candidate "Beckham or betting."

Longtime Lexington Democratic political boss Billy Klair, strongly connected with the central Kentucky racing interests, took a public position for the first time in favor of the other party's candidate, Flem Sampson, who favored betting. Sampson won.[183]

Earlier, Kentucky had established the State Racing Commission in 1906 to regulate racing.[184] It soon moved to outlaw bookmaking in favor of pari-mutuel wagering. In 1906, there were twenty-six licensed (by the track) bookies working the Kentucky Derby at Churchill Downs.[185]

Through all of this political turmoil, it is not surprising that changes were also happening at the Kentucky tracks and were centered on the Kentucky Jockey Club.

Jockey clubs were originally comprised of racehorse owners and breeders, not riders. The first in Kentucky was the Lexington Jockey Club, organized in 1797.[186] Its purpose was to "improve the breed" and bring some order to horse racing in Lexington, the town trustees having banned the practice of racing on Main Street. Henry Clay was a founding member. It built a new racetrack, the first oval in Kentucky, on property west of what is today Newtown Pike. The Lexington Jockey Club was something of a mutual association, and it made rules for what jockeys should wear, when and by whom horses could race, etc. It ceased operations and racing around 1823.[187]

In the next evolution of jockey clubs, they became stock associations, which is to say they raised capital to build tracks and facilities by the sale of shares of stock. The Kentucky Association, which succeeded the Lexington Jockey Club, was organized in 1826 and capitalized at $3,000 through the sale of shares at $50 each. A club room was established in a local hotel, the Phoenix, and only members could enter. This sanctuary would move to the association track when the clubhouse was build. Again, only members could relax in the clubhouse and watch races from there, as opposed to mingling with the crowd on the rail. Now, however, membership in the club was open to anyone who could buy a share, total membership being limited by the number of authorized shares.[188]

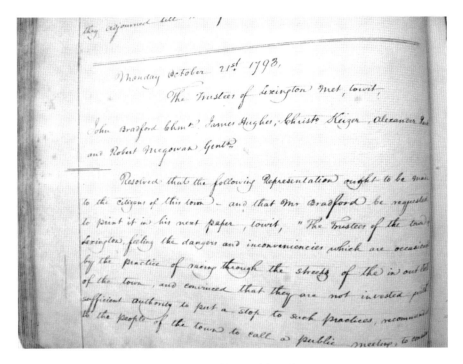

City of Lexington Trustees' Minute Book. *Photograph by author.*

As with any other enterprise, clubs and tracks had varied economic success. By 1894, the Louisville Jockey Club was deeply in debt and was sold to a syndicate of "gamblers, bookies and businessmen," thus effectively putting the foxes in charge of the henhouse.[189]

In time, it too would be sold. In 1918, a new corporation was formed called the Kentucky Jockey Club to "bring business efficiency" to racing in Kentucky and to act as a "further aid to a thoroughbred industry under siege."[190] It was capitalized by the sale of $1 million of stock to businessmen and horsemen. One major investor was both, John E. Madden.[191]

The new Kentucky Jockey Club quickly set about purchasing the state's top tracks and, if the experience of Kentucky Association shareholders is any guide, the tracks were acquired by the exchange of stock in the new entity. By the time the spring racing season was underway, the KJC owned the Lexington track, Churchill Downs, Douglas Park (also in Louisville) and Latonia (Covington) racetracks.[192] It exercised such control over Kentucky racing that it became the target of anti-trust charges, which it successfully defended.[193]

By 1927, it had added Fairmount Park in Illinois (East St. Louis), and Lincoln Fields and Hawthorne tracks, both in Chicago.[194] If it is correct that only three states permitted legal racing at this time, the Kentucky Jockey Club controlled the top tracks in two of those three states.

The Kentucky Association, Inc. was incorporated to buy back the Lexington track, but the KJC continued to operate the track.[195] The KJC was reorganized as a holding corporation called the American Turf Association, reflecting its multistate operations in 1927. During the Great Depression, all of its tracks except Churchill Downs closed, and in 1950, it became Churchill Downs, Inc.[196]

The closing down of racing in all but three states led to a tremendous drop in the value of racehorses. With few places to race and no purses to win, there was little reason to breed more horses. One exception for wealthy American horsemen was to ship their horses to England and continental Europe, where, to the consternation of the English horsemen, the American horses began to beat English thoroughbreds and win races. To make matters worse, the influx of horses flooded the English equine market and caused prices to drop.[197]

To protect both their egos and their wallets, the English responded.

Victor Albert George Child-Villiers, the seventh Earl of Jersey, was one of the stewards of the English Jockey Club, which maintained the *General Stud Book* for British and Irish horses.[198] Only horses approved for entry in the book could be called thoroughbreds in its jurisdiction. In 1913, he sponsored an amendment to the registration rules that the press nicknamed the "Jersey Act."[199] The new rule read: "No horse or mare can, after this date, be considered eligible for admission, unless it can be traced without flaw on both sire's and dam's side of its pedigree to horses and mares themselves already accepted in earlier volumes of this book."[200]

The Seventh Earl of Jersey. *National Portrait Gallery Picture Library (England).*

The American stud book was not started until 1873, many decades after the British book, and therefore many of its records for the early part of the nineteenth century were incomplete. Other records had been lost or destroyed during the Civil War. As a consequence, it was extremely difficult for most American horses to meet the "without flaw" standard and qualify for registration, relegating them to the status of "half-breeds" or worse. A horse could still race, as the Jockey Club did not govern the English tracks, but it was worthless as breeding stock.[201]

To gauge the impact of the Jersey Act, as the rule came to be known, such great horses as *Man-o-War*, Triple Crown winner *Gallant Fox* and all descendants of sixteen-year sire book champion *Lexington* were not eligible to be registered.[202] In fact, the majority of American horses were ineligible.[203] Many American horsemen began to sell their thoroughbred stock.

One of the most noted horsemen and breeders in American was John E. Madden in Lexington, Kentucky. He founded his farm, Hamburg Place, with the proceeds of the sale of his horse *Hamburg* in 1897. Within only a few years, the farm grew to more than two thousand acres.[204]

Madden was of the opinion that when others wanted to sell, he should buy. For example, in 1912, Colonel E.F. Clay, owner of the renowned Runnymeade Stud, sold his entire stock of thirty-five mares, yearlings and sucklings to Madden. Included in the sale was Clay's half interest in the stallion *Star Shoot*. Later that year, Madden acquired the other half interest in the stud.[205]

Star Shoot became the star of Hamburg Place. Having been bred only twenty-eight times in the last year of Clay's ownership, the stallion was bred ninety times by Madden. That first crop yielded fifty-two named mares and thirty-six champions. *Star Shoot* was America's leading sire for five years between 1911 and the year of his death in 1919, including champion *Sir Barton*.[206] John Madden ranked first or second as the leading breeder, both in terms of races won and money won by horses he bred from 1917 to 1928.[207]

American racing rebounded from the prohibitive laws and social attacks and was thriving again in the 1930s as laws changed and tracks opened or reopened. American racing and breeding interests continued to complain about the Jersey Act and advocate its repeal. Finally, and quietly, the British Jockey Club revoked the Jersey Act language in its regulations and substituted text that a horse "must be able to prove satisfactorily some eight or nine crosses of pure blood, to trace back for at least a century" and to "show such performances" of its family on the racetrack "as to warrant belief in the purity of its blood." This had little effect on American racing, which had risen to world dominance; but it cleared many champions and their get for inclusion in the British stud book.[208]

Civil War Racing in Lexington

L exington may hold the distinction of being the only site where racing occurred during the Civil War in Confederate-occupied territory.[209]

Kentucky officially declared neutrality when the war began, but that posture was untenable as Confederate forces soon invaded far western Kentucky and Union forces moved in from Indiana and Ohio. On September 19, 1861, the Third Kentucky Infantry (USA) marched into Lexington, to be followed the next day by the First Kentucky Cavalry (USA). They camped at the Fairgrounds, now the Student Center portion of the University of Kentucky campus, which included an eight-hundred-seat amphitheater, brick floral hall and a racetrack.[210]

While the Spring Meet for 1861 appears to have been cancelled, or perhaps begun but abandoned, due to increasing hostilities, the departing of men for one side or the other, etc., races were held in the fall. The Lexington Country Fair held four days of racing starting on September 7 at the Kentucky Association Track on the northeast edge of the city. The Kentucky Association Autumn Meet for six days started on September 23, just four days after the Union army occupied Lexington.[211]

Lexington was put under martial law, which included denial of the freedoms of speech, press and assembly. Generals ruled the community, and soldiers were posted on street corners. The Union commanders occupied the Bodley House in downtown's Gratz Park, across the park from the Hunt Morgan house, which belonged to the family of Confederate general John

Hunt Morgan. In all, at least twelve regiments camped in Lexington. Despite the occupation, or perhaps because of it, for Union sympathizers, there was an active social season during the winter, with families favoring either side hosting parties and balls.[212]

Racing continued the next June 2–9 with a full seven days of racing during the Union occupancy.[213] However, the forces of the war were moving closer to Lexington.

During August 1862, General Edmund Kirby Smith (CSA) invaded Kentucky through the Cumberland Gap and marched into central Kentucky. On August 30, he defeated a Union force of sixty-five hundred near the city of Richmond. Lexington prepared for the coming Confederate occupation, taking down Union flags and symbols while the retreating Union army destroyed ammunition and supplies.

On September 2, the Confederate force of some eleven thousand men walked into town and paraded down Main Street to the cheers of Southern-leaning citizens.[214] General Smith established his headquarters downtown in the Phoenix Hotel.[215]

Four days later, what was called an "Extra Meeting" was run for three days over the Association track.[216] There can be little doubt that General Smith, and particularly his cavalry officers, including General John Hunt Morgan, attended at least some of the races. This was to be the only meet run while the Confederacy controlled Lexington.

After the Battle of Perryville on October 8, the Confederate forces began a retreat to Tennessee. General Morgan and his cavalry fought a rearguard defense to protect the retreating infantry, riding into Lexington for a brief skirmish at Ashland, Henry Clay's former home, capturing about five hundred men and taking their guns, equipment and horses before leaving to rejoin Smith. Smith's army took freely of Lexington's citizens (as had the Northern army earlier), leaving with four thousand wagons, herds of horses, mules and cattle and sheep. Randolph Hollingsworth states that many soldiers carried off country hams affixed to their bayonets.[217]

Ambrose states that both fall and spring meets were not held in 1863,[218] although the Racing Calendars lists a three-day fall meet starting September 21.

The Association Spring Meet of four days was held in May 1864. A week later, the city saw the last war action, as Morgan conducted another raid, among other things burning some stables at the Association track. In addition to liberating all the horses and mules in local livery stables, Morgan stole a number of valuable thoroughbreds from Henry Clay's son John.[219]

Kentucky Association Race Track. *Lexington History Museum, Inc.*

It was generally viewed by those familiar with the cavalry of both sides that thoroughbred horses made the better cavalry mounts, one observer noting that when two units were sent on a hard campaign together, those riding thoroughbreds regularly wore out other breeds.[220]

The September meet that year was held in regular order for six days; Ambrose reports a large contingent of Union soldiers and officers attended.[221]

General Robert E. Lee and the Army of Northern Virginia surrendered on April 9, 1865, and the Confederate government fled Richmond, effectively ending the Civil War. Racing in Lexington continued with the Spring Meeting.

Kentucky Just *Owns* the Triple Crown

The Commonwealth of Kentucky doesn't really claim ownership of the Triple Crown races; but it can claim a very close connection with each of the races that the other tracks involved cannot.

Churchill Downs and the Kentucky Derby

The state's connection with the Kentucky Derby is well known, of course. Colonel Meriwether Lewis Clark Jr.[222] established Churchhill Downs on land he rented from two uncles, John and Henry Churchill, in 1875 and the Derby was first run that year. The one-mile elongated oval track is known for its long home stretch, with a distance from the last turn to the finish line being 1,234.5 feet.

After the bankruptcy and closure of the Woodlawn Racecourse in 1870, Louisville was without a track. Despite Louisville being the largest city in Kentucky, all the major races were held in Lexington at the Kentucky Association Course. In 1872, a group of horsemen approached Clark to see if he could fashion a solution and restart racing in Louisville. Clark had no racing experience of his own, so he left for Europe to study racing, tracks and stakes. He returned in a year with a plan to start a track with stakes races patterned after the famous English races. In particular, he proposed a Kentucky Derby fashioned after the English Epsom Derby. As reported in *The Kentucky Encyclopedia*, he told a group of horsemen that in ten years the winner of the Kentucky Derby would be worth more than the farm on which the horse was born.

The Downs initially had a small wooden grandstand on its east side, which was replaced in 1885 by a larger grandstand on the west side of the track with a seating capacity of 1,500 and standing room for another 2,000.[223] This is in great contrast to the current ability to accommodate more than 165,000 for Derby Day.[224]

The Kentucky Derby itself is a mile and one quarter long and, with one exception, has been run on the first Saturday in May since 1938. The exception was in 1945, when a wartime ban on racing was not lifted in time. That year, the Derby was held on June 9.[225]

THE PREAKNESS AND THE WOODLAWN TROPHY

The Woodlawn Vase is the trophy awarded to the winner of the Preakness each year; or, more accurately, a small-scale silver model of the Vase is awarded. The original is kept on display at the Baltimore Museum of Art between runnings of the second leg of the Triple Crown at the Pimlico course. Between 1917 and 1953, the winner actually got to take home the Vase, to be returned as a traveling trophy the next year. But by the 1950s, the Vase, thirty-six inches tall of solid silver crafted by Tiffany's, was too valuable for an owner to take the risk. Joanne Murray Vanderbilt, wife of Alfred Gwynne Vanderbilt, and the 1953 winner declined taking the Vase and instead started the tradition of the winner getting to keep a smaller replica at fourteen inches tall. The winning jockey and trainer get a slightly smaller version.[226]

So, what is the Kentucky connection?

In 1859, the Woodlawn Race Course was established on the east side of Louisville, Kentucky, near the Louisville & Frankfort Railroad for easy access by the public.[227] The track opened to great success, more than $23,000 was sold in betting pools and there was an overflow crowd. A feature of the track was a grove of trees in the infield, which obscured the horses partway through a race.[228]

In 1860, Robert A. Alexander of Woodford County, Kentucky, commissioned a "challenge vase" from Tiffany's of New York City to be presented as a traveling trophy by the Woodlawn Association. Thomas G.

The Woodlawn Vase. *Baltimore Museum of Art.*

Moore's filly *Mollie Jackson* won it the first time in 1861 and his mare *Idlewild* won it the next year, which put the Vase in Moore's possession when the Confederate army invaded Kentucky in 1862. Moore buried the Vase, together with other family silver and jewels, on his Woodford County farm for safety. After the Civil War, Moore unearthed the Vase and returned it to Woodlawn, which continued to award it until that track closed in 1870.

Now known as the Woodlawn Vase, it was awarded in 1878 at Churchill Downs for the American Stallion Stakes. The winners, from Brooklyn, took the Vase east and presented it to the Coney Island Jockey Club. Over the years, it traveled from track to track—Coney Island, Morris Park, Sheepshead Bay and Jerome Park—until finding its new home at Pimlico in 1917.[229]

The winner of the Preakness each year gets a copy of a trophy designed for and presented first at a Kentucky racetrack.

THE BELMONT STAKES AND AUGUST BELMONT

The third and final contest in the Triple Crown is the Belmont States, run at the Belmont Park each year. One might be excused for thinking the race is named for the track, but that is not the case.

August Belmont was born in what is now Germany and as a young man entered into the employ of the Rothschild banking company in Germany. In 1837, he came to New York City to serve as agent for the Rothschilds and, ultimately, start his own bank. He was one of the richest men of his day and a banker, diplomat, political leader, patron of the arts and a horseman.[230] He was among the founders of Jerome Park, a track near the Bronx, in 1867 and was president of the track association. Due to his financial support and social prestige, an early stakes race that first year was named the Belmont Stakes in his honor. In short order, Belmont had established breeding and racing stables of his own.[231]

August Belmont's Nursery Stud, Lexington (postcard). *Lexington History Museum, Inc.*

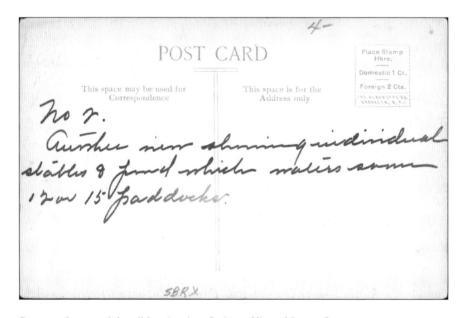

Reverse of postcard describing the view. *Lexington History Museum, Inc.*

In 1885, in a move Wall describes as adding "an entirely new dimension to the map of existing horse farms," Belmont decided to move his breeding operations from Long Island to Kentucky.[232] Belmont leased a farm on the Georgetown Road just north of Lexington and established his Nursery Stud there. Belmont's arrival in Kentucky signaled to the horsemen of the North and East that Kentucky was the place to breed and race horses and began a Bluegrass Revival, as others followed him.[233]

Belmont died in 1890; his son, also named August, bought several of his father's horses at the estate sale and continued the breeding operation at Nursery Stud as well as the family's deep involvement in thoroughbreds. Belmont II[234] eventually bred 129 stakes winners and is credited in saving horse racing in the East.

In 1905, Belmont II opened Belmont Park on Long Island, New York, naming it in his father's honor. The Belmont Stakes had continued at Jerome Park until 1889, then at Morris Park starting in 1890. This year, it was moved to the new Belmont Park track.[235]

Belmont II served in the U.S. Signal Corps during World War I and, due to his absence, decided to sell most of his 1917 crop of yearlings. One of those colts was named *My Man-o-War* by Belmont's wife in recognition of his military service. Before the 1918 Saratoga sales, Belmont dropped the first word of the name. The soon-to-be-famous *Man-o-War* sold for a "good but not spectacular price" of $5,000.[236] Belmont II continued his Kentucky operations until his death in 1924.

So, while Kentucky only has the Derby, it has a very special and unique connection with each of the other two legs of the Triple Crown.

$2 TO WIN ON NO. 5

W hen the first bet was placed on a horse, and whether it was for money, ego, status or the horse itself, is unknown. But how bets have been made over the centuries is an interesting history.

The earliest bets in the context of racing were generally considered to be between two horse owners or two other individuals.[237] Races were either quarter-mile sprints or multi-mile heats around a track. In colonial America, land was, first, too valuable and, second, too difficult to clear to devote space to an oval track. In fact, as in early Lexington, races were down existing streets or roads.

As racing became more sophisticated, jockey clubs were formed, oval tracks were established and the number of horses in a race increased (because the tracks were wide enough to do so). The rules for betting became more detailed as well.

The 1830 Rules and Regulations of the Kentucky Association in Lexington contained thirty-six paragraphs. Of these, nine, or a full 25 percent, regulated *betting*—and one prohibited *gambling*. For example, rule 24 provides that if both wagering parties are present, either may require the money be staked or shown before the race starts; if not, the bet may be voided. Or if a party betting is absent, the party present can go to the judges and declare the bet void unless some third party puts up the money wagered. On the other hand, no gambling was permitted on the grounds under control of the club, and a committee was authorized to employ police to arrest and punish anyone violating rule 34.[238]

Today, *bet*, *wager* and *gamble* are treated pretty synonymously; however, it is clear that in 1830 they had different or differing meanings. A bet or wager was considered to be a calculated and informed act by a gentleman knowledgeable about confirmation, breeding, jockey skill and other considerations that would go into deciding which horse should win. A gamble involved, and indeed might be entirely, the element of chance.

As frequently happened in the English language, there are two words for the same thing with different etymologies. *Bet* has a first known use of 1591 and may well have its origin in Saxony, in what became England.[239] *Wager* goes back to at least the fourteenth century and is derived from Anglo-French *wageure*, showing the Norman French influence on our language. While the first definition is today's common one, the archaic definition was to give one's pledge to do something and abide by the result of some action.[240] Thus, a wager was considered a promise to pay if a horse did not win.[241]

The dictionary takes a tiered process to arrive at the origin of *gamble*, referring to the word *gambler* and thence in turn to *game*, the origin of which dates to before the twelfth century and derives from Old High German and Old Norse *gaman*, pleasure or amusement.[242] In other words, a gamble was not the considered judgement of an informed man but just a game of chance and thus had no place in the track clubhouse, which was open only to members in good standing.[243]

Finally, Kentucky's current state constitution, when adopted in 1891, prohibited gambling but allowed for wagering on horse races.[244]

Bookmakers at a track. *Keeneland Library.*

This prohibition on gambling at the track only encouraged offtrack gambling. While bookmaking and bet takers operating to make a profit had been around since ancient Rome, bookmaking as a modern practice developed in England in the late eighteenth century and soon spread to the United States. The bookmaker seeks to maintain a "balanced book" of bets so that he will make a profit regardless of which horse wins.[245]

In the post–Civil War period, bookmaking in Lexington centered in its finest hotel, the Phoenix Hotel. By the 1880s, however, criminal elements were entering the picture and forming "betting rings" around the country. Not only were these "pernicious influences" sullying the pure wagering of gentlemen, they were also diverting money from the operation of the tracks. The Kentucky Association in Lexington amended its charter to permit Association-operated betting on the grounds of the track and at one place off the track as designated by the Association—no doubt that place was the Phoenix. The Association issued a public call to all tracks in the United States to do the same.[246]

Bookies and bookmaking now entered the track grounds, but it was not a pretty sight. They were described as being littered about the track grounds, their runners plying members of the crowd to go bet, running to the stables for any information and rushing back to their bookie, who could adjust his odds. Some stood under umbrellas to identify their location to bettors; sometimes the track would erect a tent to corral the bookies in one place.[247] The 1894 new grandstand at Churchill Downs included twenty stalls for bookmakers.[248]

The grandest "bookie enclosure" in the country was Floral Hall at Lexington's Red Mile. It is sometimes called the "round barn," because horses were stalled there at times, even though it is an octagonal brick structure. Built on the community fairgrounds in 1882 as a floral display and exhibit facility, its center is open so judges could view all the exhibits on three levels and compare entries easily. Trotting-horse races began at the adjoining track in 1875; eventually, the Kentucky Trotting Horse Breeders Association acquired the track and Floral Hall. Betting followed the races, of course. When Lexington outlawed gambling inside the city limits in the late 1800s, the bookies had to leave the downtown hotels. Floral Hall, however, was just outside the city boundary; the track itself was not. The bookies moved their operations into the hall.[249]

The Kentucky Association adopted a similar strategy. While half of the track was inside the city limits, the final turn and home stretch were not, and the association built its "betting shed" near the final turn.[250]

Bookmakers in the clubhouse. *Keeneland Library.*

Floral Hall, Lexington. *Photograph by author.*

Bookies would travel from track to track following the racing circuit. They began to form associations that would negotiate arrangements with tracks on their behalf. In 1891, for example, the Kentucky Association reached an agreement with the Western Bookmakers' Association whereby the track was to be paid between $18,000 and $20,000 for allowing the Bookmaker's Association to send fifteen to twenty bookies for the twelve-day spring meet.[251]

License fees and group deals were a good source of revenue not only for tracks. Individual bookmakers also could make serious money, particularly as they could become the favorite bookie for wealthy men and breeders, who would favor one man over the others. Bookmaker Robert G. Irving made $93,000 in 1887, for example, and George A. Wheelock netted $143,000 in 1888 after paying winning bets. Charles Riley Grannan from Paris, Kentucky, could sometimes make $20,000 to $30,000 on a single race.[252]

Raymond W. Kanzler wrote a retrospective for the *Baltimore Sun* in 1958 describing his experience with bookies at Pimlico. "They were gentlemen," he wrote. "They dressed, spoke, drank and behaved in general like gentlemen." Perhaps he was describing those bookies in the clubhouse. The bigger bookmakers had runners who scampered about the track seeking information on horses and jockeys, takers who calculated and recalculated odds, writing them on chalkboards behind the bookie and ticket writers to write out a betting slip for a patron. Bookmakers with more limited resources watched the odds boards of the larger operations and copied them.[253]

This method of betting is known as fixed-odds betting, in that the odds are agreed upon by bookie and bettor when the bet is placed, regardless of how the odds may change until the race is run. In contrast is pari-mutuel betting, in which the final payout, and odds, are not determined until betting on a race closes. Thus a bettor may place a bet with 4–1 odds, only to find the odds drop to 2–1 at race time as others place bets on the same horse.[254]

The pari-mutuel system of betting was invented by a Frenchman named Pierre Oller and introduced in Paris, France, around 1780. As opposed to betting against the bookie, a bettor wagers against all other bettors. At the conclusion of a race, the track takes its percentage, and the balance of the pool of money is divided by the total number of successful wagers. The beauty of the system is that the track knows it will get revenue, which can increase as the volume and amount of bets increase (as opposed to a fix fee from bookie associations), and any number of people can bet on the winning horse (as opposed to bookies, who stop taking bets on a particular horse to balance the book).[255] As the progressive forces of social reform succeeded in outlawing bookmaking, the pari-mutual system was ready to take its place. Pari-mutual wagering was approved by the Kentucky General Assembly in 1918, although tracks had started using the system earlier.[256]

Keeping track of the bets and changing odds required manpower, as the early tallies were kept on chalkboards at the track. As popularity, and legality, increased, small machines—essentially early adding machines— were manufactured to do the work, and in big tracks were ganged to keep up and the machines began to be grouped in small buildings of their own. It was time for automation.

There are different stories on who invented the automatic totalisator machine. Kristina Panos gives credit to an Australian engineer, George Julius, who was actually trying to invent an election vote calculator, with the first commercial machine being installed at a New Zealand track in 1913.[257] The American Totalisator Company, on the other hand, credits its founder and engineer Harry Straus and a group of American engineers with inventing and installing the first electromechanial system at Arlington Park in 1933.[258]

It may be the distinction that the Julius system was purely mechanical and operated like a complex grandfather clock, with levers and weights. When a bet was made, the betting agent would pull a level that tugged at one of many overhead wires. Each pull represented a bet. The wires adjusted wheels and gears that turned large wheels with numbers on them, which were visible through second-floor windows of a two-story betting house. The New Zealand betting house had thirty betting windows and thirty betting agents pulling levers for bets and horses.[259]

The ritual incantation "$2 to win on no. 5" had its beginnings with the functional limitations of these early mechanical systems. The data had to be entered in a precise order: dollar amount, place, horse. If a bettor gave the information to the teller in the wrong order, the teller had to wait and then enter it in the correct order or the bet would not register. There were limited opportunities to enter preset dollar amounts, usually two, five, ten and twenty dollars. A six-dollar bet, for example, was impossible. A bettor would have to make three two-dollar bets. Larger bets were taken at special windows. Even though most tracks paid the horses through fourth place in a race, the machine could handle only three places. Computing power had to be reserved for the unknown number of entries in a race, which was governed by the width of the track and the number of stalls in the starting gate.

The AmTote machine was operated by electricity, not levers and weights. AmTote also claims invention of the first automated totalisator system, the first dash/sell terminal, the first Windows-based tote system and, as of 2013, was venturing into wireless terminals, voice betting, Internet betting and Instant Racing—all of the modern, computer-driven betting systems and devices familiar to betters today. These innovations also made possible the almost infinite variations of betting among horses, places and amounts known as "exotic wagering."[260]

My Old Kentucky Track

This chapter looks at, and for, the former Kentucky tracks that once thrilled to the pounding hooves of racing horses and the cheers of anxious bettors. It will not discuss the Kentucky racetracks that are in operation as of 2017. According to one researcher, there were at least twenty-two tracks in operation at one time or another prior to the Civil War, and at least another seven tracks in operation afterward that have closed.[261] This list, however, is not complete. It was from a single source, and other research has revealed tracks not in the compilation. In fact, it is not certain that every racetrack, especially in the period prior to 1800, has been rediscovered.

The First Track(s)

There are several contenders for the label "the first race track in Kentucky." Early races were typically between two horses only and over a quarter-mile straight track, often a road. As Kentucky's settlements evolved and land could be cleared, wider oval tracks came into use, permitting more horses to race at the same time.[262] Also at this time, the threat of Indian attacks had to be eliminated. Thornton notes that at the end of a quarter-mile race near Shallow Ford Station in Mercer County in 1781, an Indian rose up out of the canebrake and shot the winning rider. He also states that there were three

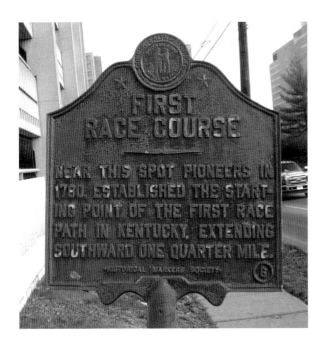

Kentucky Historic Marker of "First Race Course." *Photograph by the author.*

quarter-mile straight tracks between Harrodsburg and Boonesboro by 1782, which is to say, between the forts at those locations.[263] A state historic marker at the top of the hill in the 300 block of South Broadway in Lexington states that it is located near the starting point for the first "race path" in Kentucky.[264] The path, again, was a quarter-mile straight track running south. It should be noted that South Broadway is also Harrodsburg Road and thus in the shadow of the fort's protection roughly thirty miles away. William Perrin states that Broadway was not "opened" until 1786, but as it was the way to Fort Harrod, there must have been some path.[265]

EARLY TRACKS

An interesting and often repeated story is that of Colonel William Whitley, who established a track in Crab Orchard, Kentucky. It was the first oval track in the state and situated such that it encircled a small hill from which patrons could watch the horses run. Whitley was considered a philanthropist, patriot, poet and hero and was paid for his military service in land. At one time, he owned thousands of acres in Kentucky. Crab Orchard is on the

Wilderness Trail from Cumberland Gap to Danville, about forty miles south of Lexington.[266] English racetracks ran a race clockwise around a tract. Whitley was so anti-English that he started the American practice of running races counterclockwise to avoid imitating his former enemy.[267] He was also a noted Indian fighter, having fought in some twenty engagements, including the one near Detroit in which he died in 1813.

A resort opened in Crab Orchard in the early 1800s that, in addition to a racetrack, featured a golf course, lake, poolroom, bowling alley, a dining room that could seat almost four hundred people and 250 hotel rooms. The Great Depression was a large factor in its demise.[268]

When Robert Sanders settled on his one-thousand-acre tract between Georgetown and Lexington in 1790, the area was still part of Fayette County. Two years later, it would be part of the newly formed Scott County. Sanders was wealthy and a horseman. By 1793, he was operating the county's first racetrack and breeding thoroughbreds. Three more years later, he had built a five-hundred-bed hotel and tavern on his farm for the convenience of race-going guests.[269] His meets were regularly advertised in the Lexington newspapers. Even though Sanders died in 1805, his sons evidently continued his equine and hospitality empire with races advertised as late as 1815.[270]

A late, great and short-lived addition to Kentucky racing was Raceland in Greenup County, known as the "Million Dollar Oval" for the expense to which Jack Keene and the Tri-State Fair and Racing Association went to build the track near Ashland in 1922. The association bought land from Keene and made him the general manager.[271] A lake occupied the infield, and white fences faced with rosebushes lined the course.[272] Its first race, the Ashland Handicap, was held on July 10, 1924, with 27,000 in attendance in the elaborate grandstand. By 1928, the association was behind in payment of a daily fee to the Commonwealth of Kentucky for the license to race; state authorities arrived to seize cash on hand. That left the track unable to make its mortgage payment, and the bank foreclosed. After it was sold in 1928, the new owners tried for several years to operate it as a fairgrounds, but, eventually, it closed permanently.[273]

In addition to the foregoing tracks, the following cities and counties in Kentucky had racetracks between 1800 and 1860: Glasgow, Camp Nelson, Maysville, Bardstown, Sharpsburgh, Eminence, Hopkinsville, Owensboro, Newport, Greensburgh, Elkhorn, Cynthiana, Burksville, Falmouth, Keysburg, Logan, Richmond, Russellville, Harrodsburg, Versailles, Henderson and Paducah,[274] as well as Frankfort, Winchester, Shepherdsville, Harrodsburg, Columbia and Bethlehem in Henry County.[275]

LEXINGTON TRACKS

To say that there was a racetrack on every block of early Lexington would not be entirely accurate; but it would not be far from the truth.

The first racetrack in Lexington was not an officially sanctioned track. In fact, officials disapproved.

The custom had begun of racing on Main Street.

It is not known whether the practice was the result of any organized group. Thornton notes that Perrin's 1882 *History of Fayette County* reports that a James Bray opened a tavern near the present Jefferson Street, which had been on the western edge of the town, and began running races.[276]

The Lexington Jockey Club was organized in 1787 to conduct races on an organized basis and according to its rules. Its races were run on the town Commons, a strip of land along the Town Branch, the middle fork of the Elkhorn River.[277] One historian reports that the first race conducted by the club was held in October 1789 according to the "rules of New Market [*sic*]" (England).[278] But if someone wanted to race and didn't want to conform to the club's rules, or wanted to race horses that didn't meet the entry criteria, or the club was not conducting a formal meet at the time, there was always Main Street.

Lexington was formally chartered as a town under Virginia law by that General Assembly on May 6, 1782, providing for a board of trustees to govern the town, lay off streets and other powers.[279] In 1790, the trustees approved the repurchase of two lots of land along Town Branch and the sale of unappropriated land at the east end of town to provide funds to pay for the land and to pay for "digging a canal to carry the branch straight through the town, also to have a row of lively locust trees planted on each side of the canal."[280] This provided a much better venue for horse racing. The hillside rising up from across the stream provided a good vantage point for spectators.

On October 21, 1793, the board of trustees for Lexington met to discuss the practice of horse racing on Main Street, which the trustees viewed as a "growing evil" and, considering that they were without sufficient authority to ban the practice without citizen support, passed a resolution calling for a public vote.[281] Evidently, the votes favored a change, for on December 21, 1793, the trustees approved another resolution prohibiting the "running or racing of horses in the streets or highways within the limits of said town," prohibited the showing of stud horses in same, established a schedule of fines for violations and relegated the stud horses to part of Water Street, along the

City of Lexington Trustees' Minute Book. *Photograph by author.*

Town Branch creek west of Cross Street (Broadway).[282] Racing was formally moved to the town Commons along the stream. Evidently, Lexington was not alone with this problem, for in 1793, the Kentucky legislature passed a statue banning horse races in streets.[283]

Illegal racing evidently continued, however, and the trustees on March 21, 1795, again considered a proposed law banning Main Street racing.[284]

To put this all in context, Lexington had a population of only 850 people in 1790.[285]

As noted earlier, a straight course for racing had been established on what is now South Broadway in the early 1780s, outside the platted town boundaries. Lexington's formal town limits were platted in 1791, and its southern (southwestern) line was near present-day Maxwell Street, about where the Broadway tract started.[286] By the time the plat was filed, however, racing interests had recognized the antipathy of the town trustees and moved outside the town limits.

Some time during the 1770s or early 1780s, Colonel John Todd conducted racing, likely another straight race path, on his property along the road to Georgetown, just west of Lexington, between today's Short and Third Streets. Todd was the great uncle of Mary Todd, who married Abraham Lincoln. Unfortunately, Colonel Todd died in the Battle of Blue Licks in 1783. A widower, he left a young daughter as his only living heir; interest in racing there ended. As Lexington grew toward Todd lands and the property was subdivided and sold as house lots, the deeds frequently referred to the greater property as "the Old Race Field."[287]

The Lexington Jockey Club now wanted to build an oval track, as the mile-long heats races that tested endurance were becoming more popular than the quarter-mile sprints focused on speed.

It constructed, or caused to be constructed, an oval track on a large and fairly flat piece of land farther west from Todd on the other side of the Georgetown Pike in what is now the rear of the Lexington Cemetery and extending north in what is today a small residential neighborhood. Races were conducted as early as 1795.[288] This course was a one-mile oval and went by several names: the Williams (or Williams Brothers) Course, Boswells' Woods and Lee's Woods;[289] but when the Jockey Club conducted its contests, it referred to them as being run on the "Lexington Course," which may have been a designation of the racecourse itself as distinct from the total property.[290] An advertisement announcing a forthcoming race in October 1795 noted, among other information, that horses were to be entered by the day before the race or pay a double fee to enter on race day.[291] Ambrose reports that the Jockey Club ceased conducting race meets by 1823.[292]

For a year in the midst of this period, 1800, Sollow has compiled some interesting statistics. Among the heads of households in Kentucky, 92 percent reported owning at least one horse, and two-thirds had two or more horses. The average stable of a taxpayer was three horses; the number increased to four for landowners other than town lots, and slaveholders reported an average of five horses.[293]

In the early 1810s, there were races at the "Pond Course," listed in one advertisement as being two miles from Lexington, but the compass direction is not given.[294] One writer speculates it may have been on a farm two to three miles northeast of Lexington on the Maysville Road, now Paris Pike, known locally at the time as Wrights Pond or "the Pond." Wright maintained a tavern and frequently held barbecues, music festivals and other events to increase the business in his tavern.[295]

Between 1823 and 1826, racing meets were held on private racing tracks around Lexington, including Henry Clay's Ashland Farm.[296]

Another track during this period was at Fowler's Garden. Opened by 1817 by Captain John Fowler, a local businessman, it lay on the east side of Lexington. Hollingsworth says it was about twenty-five acres in size.[297] J. Winston Coleman, on the other hand, says it covered between fifty and seventy-five acres.[298] Both agree that it had a racetrack, stables and related buildings, as well as facilities for fairs, livestock shows, political rallies, entertainments and exhibits "of all kinds." Hollingsworth locates the facility between Main and Fifth Streets (south and north) and Walton Avenue on the east on to Race Street on the west. Being on the east edge of town, it was more accessible then the Williams track, and it became the social center of Lexington, one writer describing it as the "fashionable Country Club of its day" with dinners and dances. She notes that Town Branch flowed through the property as well and that the community celebrated the fiftieth anniversary of independence there.[299] Hollingsworth notes that Fowler's Garden closed around 1860.

In April 1826, members of the old Jockey Club met at Mrs. Keene's Inn to start a new racing association. They entered into a subscription agreement to capitalize the new entity and agreed to conduct a preparatory race meet that June. Sixty subscribers paid fifty dollars each for one share in the new Kentucky Association for the Improvement of the Breeds of Domestic Stock. On June 8, a three-day meet began, running over the old Lexington Course. The race the first day was a three-mile run, the second day a two-miler and the third day more than one mile, with the horse carrying the best of the three wins as the purse winner. The third day also saw a "handycap" race. Over a great distance, age and weight carried mattered little; but on a shorter course, different weights (typically lead bars in saddlebags) were assigned according to the age of the horses.[300]

The Kentucky Association held its August race meet in 1826 at the Williams track, and racing appears to have continued there through 1830; but it also appears clear that the Association intended from the start to develop a new track under its ownership.[301]

The reason for that decision is not clear. It could simply be a desire to own the land. There does not seem to have been any disagreement with the owners of the Williams track as racing there was permitted for four years. There may have been some geographic defect or defect in course design; but in all events, it appears the search for a new site began early.

On July 7, 1828, the Association purchased more than fifty-seven acres from John Postlethwaite on the northeastern edge of town, at the east end of Fifth Street, close to the northernmost platted street. This site would be much more accessible to the residents of Lexington.[302] The purchase was an "insider" transaction, as it would be known today, since John Postlethwaite was both the seller (with his wife) and a member of the board of trustees for the Association. However, his ownership was publicly known, and the price must have been fair for the other trustees to agree.

A week later, on July 15, the Association purchased all or a part of Out Lot 18 within the city limits. Described as twenty poles by forty poles, the lot was 330 feet by 660 feet at the south end of town and lay the entire length of Lexington from the new track site.[303] The intended use of the lot is unknown, and Ambrose does not mention it. In the Lexington platting scheme, small in-lots were clustered around the Commons and were intended for residences, while the out-lots were intended, at least at first, to be agricultural, where residents would grow crops or keep stock. The Town Branch flowed through the lot; perhaps it was intended as pasture and corral for horses coming to race.

That summer, construction began on the new, one-mile oval track laid out in a modern flat design. Spring of 1829 saw the first races. A grandstand was erected in the center of the infield the following year with a view of the entire track, and the first formal meet was held in 1831. Admittance to the track was free, but admittance to the grandstand (and no doubt the reason for placing it in the infield) was a twenty-five-cent charge.

In 1834, an adjoining ten-acre parcel was purchased for the track, and in July 1836, four more acres were added, bringing the area to more than sixty-five acres. The Association enclosed the entire property with a wood-plank fence.[304]

The location of the Kentucky Association racetrack would have been just east or northeast of Fowler's Garden, and Hollingsworth implies that the KA track became the focus of horse races while the garden stopped races and focused more on being the community entertainment center and fairgrounds.

Racing continued at the Kentucky Association course through 1898, including one meet held while the Confederate army occupied Lexington; but a national financial panic, the opening of competing tracks and financial problems caused the track to close. For several years, crops were grown in the infield and certain trainers leased the track as a training facility.

In October 1903, Captain Samuel S. Brown from Pittsburgh purchased the property and began a series of improvements. The first grandstand was torn down to open the infield, as were many sheds and outbuildings along the back side. A new grandstand with a two-thousand-spectator capacity was built along (and outside) the home stretch, and the clubhouse was substantially renovated. A new paddock barn with fourteen stalls was added as well as a "betting shed" that had stations for up to sixty bookmakers.

The moribund Association revived and held its first race at the new facility in May 1905 with a six-day meet.

By 1907, Brown had died and the Association, newly reorganized, purchased the property from his estate. Admission was one dollar for gentlemen and half that for ladies; daily programs were ten cents. The next year, the pari-mutuel wagering system was introduced to the track.

Racing continued into the 1930s, but financial pressures resulting from the Great Depression forced its closure, with the last race run in 1933. Negotiations over several months resulted. In 1935, the federal government purchased the land for just over $67,000 for use as a federally funded housing project, and buildings and equipment were auctioned to the public.

At this same time, thoroughbred owners and breeders, deeming the old track too expensive to revive, withdrew and formed a new association. After purchase of the Keene farm on Versailles Road, it called itself the Keeneland Association and began development of the present Keeneland Race Course. As a lasting connection with the past, Keeneland purchased the old Kentucky Association gates for its entrance and adopted the "KA" logo of the old association as its own.

In 1850, the newly formed Kentucky Agricultural & Mechanical Association was incorporated in Lexington for the purpose of holding annual fairs, exhibitions, livestock shows and, with yet another track, racing and trotting meets. It purchased land south of the Maxwell Springs property on the south side of Lexington between the present Limestone and Rose Streets.[305] This sounds very much like the activities carried on at Fowler's Garden and suggests that this new track and exhibit area may have replaced Fowler's Garden and led to its closure.

An 1877 map of Lexington shows the former Fowler's Garden area as having been subdivided, the Kentucky Association track as partly within and partly without the city limits, by then a radius of one mile from the courthouse (thus permitting gambling outside the boundary), and the "Lexington Trotting Park" in the southeast corner. This track was operated by the Lexington Trotting Club, which was established in a meeting at the Phoenix Hotel in 1853.[306] The Maxwell Spring property is labeled as the "City Park."[307] Although the Red Mile Trotting Track was established in 1875, it is not shown, nor is Herr Park, which would be outside the city limits.

A remarkable one-man story lies just south of a historic section of Lexington and across from the University of Kentucky, where there was

Lexington Fairgrounds. *Frank Leslie's Illustrated Newspaper, Lexington History Museum, Inc.*

once a farm called Forest Park. The land lay just outside the mid-nineteenth-century city limits of a one-mile radius from the courthouse but inside of the first tollbooth on the way from Lexington to Nicholasville.[308] According to an 1891 map of Lexington and Fayette County surveyed by W.R. Wallis, which shows, inter alia, tollbooth locations, the booth appears to have been approximately where the present Cooper Drive intersects with South Limestone, although there were no crossroads in the vicinity at this time. The map does show Virginia Avenue almost at the city limits but close enough thereto that no farm would exist between the street and the line. Therefore, Forest Park was between today's Virginia Avenue and Cooper Drive, north and south, respectively, and Limestone Street and the railroad, east and west.[309]

In 1851, a veterinarian originally from Canada named Dr. Lee Herr came to Paris, Kentucky, to begin his practice in horse country. At some point, he began owning and trading in trotting horses and developing his own ideas about breeding and training, using the public roads of Bourbon County as his training tracks because there were no trotting tracks in the United States yet.[310] Just after the Civil War ended, Herr sold one of his horses for the then large sum of $10,000 and used his proceeds to buy Forest Park and move to Lexington.

Based on Forest Park, Herr expanded his breeding training program, while maintaining his practice (which kept him in good contact with other horsemen) and built the first trotting track on his farm. A writer for the *Lexington Leader* credits Herr with "introducing into the state the trotting horse" and notes that "there was no man in the state who had established a trotting stable for schooling trotters for track purposes until Dr. Herr."[311]

Not only did he use his track for training, Herr at least as early as 1866 also began holding trots races on his farm and inviting the public and other competitors.[312] This was, of course, a convenient way to advertise his horses and train them under actual race conditions. An article in the Lexington newspaper in 1872, at perhaps the peak point of trotting races at the Herr Track (the Red Mile Trotting Track was not established until 1875), reported: "Pretty soon the fine horses began to arrive with their fine looking drivers sitting behind them in shining, dainty looking buggies. There was no bell to tap, no officer to order up the horses, as it was simply a meeting of young gentlemen to see who of them had the best horse, and amuse themselves and each other by driving in a trotting race on which no money was bet and no pools were sold."

The article reports that there were five entries, and due to the narrow width of the track, only three could line up in the first rank and the other two behind. Just as they lined up to start, a "herd of mares" ran across the track. As the reporter mentions that two entries contended for first place "all the way around," it can be taken that it was an oval track. There were two heats run with the same entries. After the races, the drivers repaired to town, no doubt for a celebration.[313]

Unlike the Kentucky Association races, which followed something of an annual schedule of spring and fall meets, racing at Forest Park seems to have occurred whenever there was interest. Just the next month, the same newspaper reported on more trotting races at the Herr Track, noting that they had become weekly events attended by the public that afforded "pleasant amusement to our young men, without being demoralizing in their tendency."[314] In that case, the first race was the best of three one-mile heats and the second the best of five one-mile heats, thus giving the length of Herr Track from start to finish.

Racing continued at least into the 1880s, but by 1884, one of Dr. Herr's sons published an announcement for a turkey shoot at Forest Park.[315]

Dr. Herr died in 1891, and his will provided that all of his property be sold, which was conducted on the premises over two days. The stock and land were auctioned the first day and the personal property and house contents the second. A large crowd attended. The land was in two sections. The main farm (and likely the track) of 163 acres was sold first, followed by a 50-acre plot "next to the city."[316] Heretofore the location of Forest Park and the Herr Track has only been located between South Limestone Street and the railroad track outside of the Lexington city limits. However, the street and railroad track parallel each other to the county line and leave many acres of possibilities. The newspaper article announcing the auction, however, gives an important clue that leads to the actual location of the farm. The article states that the farm is "inside" or town side of the first tollbooth. That information was important to potential bidders and the estate, because it announced that no one would have to pay a toll to attend the auction. It also sets an outer limit to the farm location.

The 1891 Wallis Map of Fayette County locates the toll stations.[317] A cellphone application marries maps with global positioning system (GPS) and has done so with the Wallis Map. By traveling over relevant roads in the

Kentucky Association Track gate post at Keeneland Race Course. *Bill Straus.*

vicinity of the indicated station, it has been determined that the toll station stood approximately at the intersection of South Limestone and an interior University of Kentucky road called Farm Road, just slightly south of the present Cooper Drive.[318]

Dr. Herr's heirs bought both tracts. Within two years, the fifty acres had been subdivided into residential lots with the street named after Lexington's newspapers—Leader, Press, Transcript and Gazette—perhaps in a bid to get more publicity from the press.[319]

The 1907 Sanborn Map of Lexington shows the Association thoroughbred track on the northeast corner of the city and the Red Mile Trotting track on the southwest, and all tracks previously described developed into residential or business purposes.[320]

In addition to the racing tracks, either publicly or privately owned, many breeders and trainers had tracks on their farm used for their own purposes. Henry Clay's track at Ashland Farm is described in the chapter on Clay and the Madden family track on Hamburg Place in the chapter on Forgotten Farms as representative samples of private tracks.

Louisville Tracks

As happened in Lexington and other communities where the desire to race outpaced the development of racetracks, races in Louisville were first conducted on a downtown street, in this instance Market Street as early as 1783, just five years after George Rogers Clark founded the town.[321] Likely this was the early quarter-mile straight track type of race. It is not reported when racing on Market Street was discontinued nor what town officials thought of the practice, but certainly by the time the state law banning racing in the streets of towns was passed in 1793, it would have been discouraged.

There also appears to have been racing on a track near the end of Sixteenth Street called the Hope Distillery Course with multi-mile heats running in at least the 1820s. Races were also held at the grounds of the Louisville Agricultural Society in the 1830s, near the present site of the Louisville Water Company.[322]

A racecourse had been constructed at Shippingport, a peninsula jutting into the Ohio River just slightly downriver from the new town by 1805.[323] Shippingport as a community was chartered in 1785,[324] so it is possible the impetus for a racetrack resulted in racing there at an earlier date than 1805, again, potentially as a result of the state law.

To a Louisville citizen or visitor today, it is unimaginable that a racetrack could be built on what is now Shippingport Island at the Falls of the Ohio with the falls on the river side of the island and the Louisville and Portland Canal with its dam and locks on the town side; but when Shippingport was established, the canal had not been dug and would not be for fifty years. In the beginning, Shippingport and its ship docks was the departure point for goods sent south to New Orleans and coming north on the Ohio, just as the town of Louisville performed the same function for river traffic coming south on the Ohio or going north. Shippingport, in fact, almost eclipsed Louisville in community size and volume of business as Kentucky's most important port. A six-story flour mill was built there in 1817 and the Napoleon Distillery located there.[325] It also had the advantage of being outside Louisville city limits and any ban on gambling on horse races.

The track was a part of the Elm Tree Garden, which featured a platform three hundred feet in circumference encircling a large elm tree with a tavern. It overlooked mazes and puzzle gardens and, of course, the racetrack. It is easy to imagine a great day at the races, lingering at a table outside the tavern on the platform, watching the horses run with the Falls of the Ohio as a background. The community also had a three-story hotel with large balconies off the rooms.

Progress, however, was the demise of the Elm Tree Track. The digging of the canal in 1825 cut off the new island from the mainland and allowed ships to bypass its Shippingport's dock facilities. The community went into decline along with its businesses. When Louisville incorporated as a city in 1828, it included the former Shippingport community within its bounds. Further widening of the canal over time (today at five hundred feet) and the erection of an electric plant took more land, and the flood of 1937 devastated the area. The federal government acquired all private land in 1958 in the final expansion of the canal and functionally ended Shippingport as a community.

Before its end, however, Elm Tree Race Track produced a famous jockey of its own. Jim Porter was born there in 1810 and was a thin, sickly child. As a result, at age fourteen, his weight was low enough to allow him to become a jockey. For three years, he rode at Elm Tree. Then, at seventeen, he experienced a growth spurt, which left him at seven feet, eight inches tall, NBA size for the early 1800s and very much too big to continue riding competitively. He became famous as "The Kentucky Giant" and, trading on his fame, opened a tavern near the canal, being successful enough to build an eighteen-room house with ten-foot-tall doors and personally sized furnishings.[326]

These various efforts to establish a local track resulted in the creation of the Louisville Association for the Improvement of the Breed of Horses, which copied the Lexington entity's rules and bylaws, holding its first meeting at Washington Hall on November 5, 1831. A committee was appointed to locate land for a racetrack. A year later, just over fifty-one acres were purchased at what is now Seventh and Magnolia Streets, but which in 1832 was well away from the town. A large grove of oak trees on the property led to the new facility being called Oakland.[327]

When the first race was held the following year, Oakland Race Course was considered "one of the most handsome sporting venues in the country, welcoming even the ladies with a furnished room and private pavilion."[328]

The "greatest race west of the Alleghenies" was held at Oakland on September 30, 1839. Promoter Yelvefton C. Oliver arranged a match race between *Wagner*, an 1834 colt out of Virginia who dominated racing in the South at this time, and *Grey Eagle*, who was foaled in Lexington in 1835 and who had run the fastest two miles in the United States. The purse was a stunning $14,000 to the winner. An estimated ten thousand people attended, including Henry Clay. The hotels and lodging houses were filled to overflowing, and even the branches of the oak trees were packed.

The race was two one-mile heats, and *Wagner* won both. A rematch was called for and run five days later at the same track for a $10,000 purse. This time, each horse won a heat; but *Grey Eagle* broke down in the second heat, ending his racing career. Both horses went on to successful careers at stud, and their progeny continued their competition. Cato, the enslaved African American jockey who rode *Wagner* to victory, was given his freedom for his successes.[329]

Racing continued at Oakland Race Course through the 1840s, but after 1850, there is no further mention of the track in Louisville newspapers and it was closed.[330] The grounds served as a campground and cavalry remount station for the Union army during the Civil War and thereafter fell into disrepair.[331]

References have been found to two other early Louisville tracks, but very little information is readily available. Beargrass Creek Race Track ran from as early as 1808[332] to at least 1823. John James Audubon famously attended a July Fourth celebration at the park that involved horse races and much eating and drinking. W.S. Vosburgh mentions that Greenland Race Track existed in Louisville but was "never popular" and abandoned around 1869.[333]

The Woodlawn Race Course has already been mentioned in the chapter about the Triple Crown races in the context that the Pimlico Race trophy was originally the prize for winning the feature race at Woodlawn. The track was established near the Louisville and Frankfort Railroad in 1859 for easy access of guests to the track from the train.[334] In 1858, a flag-stop station was constructed at Woodlawn, and passengers were charged fifty cents for a nonstop ride to the track. Even after Woodlawn track closed, the railroad operated the stop until all stops were eliminated about 1935.[335]

There are few descriptions of the facilities at Woodlawn. The clubhouse is said to have been built with thick brick walls, the rooms were spacious, and there were ornate mantelpieces. The clubhouse is shown on a map in 1858 near where Ashland and Perryman Roads are today. There is a small (and telling) burial ground for African American jockeys who died as a result of racing accidents.

The *Louisville Daily Courier* reported that the spring meet in 1862 was cancelled due to "bad management." By fall, however, "important alterations" had been made to the facilities and a new agreement was made to bring food and drink to the meet, perhaps correcting the aforesaid management problems. The Civil War was raging, and the Woodlawn track was soon affected. After the Battle of Perryville on October 8, 1863, near Richmond and east of Lexington, wounded Union soldiers were transported all the way to Louisville. Woodlawn Race Course became a camp and mustering-out post for soldiers. John Scheer states that racing was "reasonably uninterrupted" by the war, which seems a hopeful statement that would still leave Lexington's Kentucky Association track as the only one to conduct regular race meets during the conflict.[336]

After the war, Woodlawn was a popular locale not only for horse racing but also for fairs and political rallies. It may even have contributed to driving the Greenland Course out of business in 1869. Interest in horse racing was waning in Louisville, though, and even Woodlawn had to close in 1870. There would follow a five-year gap when there was no active racetrack in Louisville.[337] Today, the area of the former track is part of the city of Woodlawn Park.

While Churchill Downs was conducting thoroughbred racing at its track, Colonel James J. Douglas established Douglas Park as a venue for pacing and trotting horses in 1895. He selected property near the present Standiford Field Airport and constructed a one-mile oval track with banked turns, a large grandstand rivalling that of Churchill Downs, stables and a clubhouse.

He timed its opening meet to occur when the national Grand Army of the Republic held its convention in Louisville.[338]

The track infield featured extensive flowerbeds and a lake. The feature race each year was the Kentucky Handicap, and the winner's name was spelled out in flowers in the infield.[339]

Douglas Park enjoyed success at the start with its trotting and pacing races, but by 1906, is was forced to close. Six years later, it reopened as a thoroughbred venue. In 1918, Churchill Downs acquired Douglas Park and converted it into an exercise and training facility. Over the years, demolition removed some buildings, others were destroyed by fire. Churchill began selling off portions of the Douglas property in the 1950s; by the end of that decade, all equine-related activity had ceased.[340]

Henry Clay, Horse Breeder and Racer

Henry Clay, well known as the Great Compromiser, was the politician and statesman who almost single-handedly preserved the Union from early division and, in some estimates, pushed back the eventual Civil War over slavery thirty years. He ran for president five times and famously said, "I'd rather be right than president."

But outside of a comparatively small covey of Clay cognoscente, his expertise and extensive involvement in breeding and racing thoroughbreds at his home estate of Ashland is little known. His principle biographers mention his involvement with horses but downplay his role.

David and Jeanne Heidler, for example, set forth his growing number of horses owned from the tax rolls between 1799, when he owned two horses—likely for personal use—and 1808, when he owned more than thirty horses, by then clearly in excess of those needed for personal transportation. Indeed, they note that the increase was reflective of "a growing passion" for horse racing, but they give the statistics more to demonstrate Clay's increase in income and wealth than as a comment on his entry into the horse business.[341]

In Robert Remini's extensive biography of Henry Clay,[342] a painful search of the index reveals no entries for horses or horse racing. Instead, the short relevant entry is found under "Henry Clay, characteristics, as cattleman and farmer."[343] Instructive of the treatment of Clay as horseman is the following:

Clay also experimented with sugar beets and different grasses for pasture only to decide that the native bluegrass occupied a superior class by itself.

In addition, the farm produced some tobacco, corn, wheat and rye....Hogs, goats, cows, mules, and horses were raised by the hundreds at Ashland.... Over the next several years he began to breed Maltese jackasses, Arabian horses, Saxon and merino sheep, and English Hereford and Durham cattle. He imported cattle from abroad, and his racehorses were so superior and earned him so much prize money that Clay built a private racetrack at Ashland.[344]

It is understandable that Clay's biographers wanted to focus more on his political and diplomatic career, and to a lesser extent on his family; but burying his extensive equine activity among the hogs, mules and sheep does not give a true portrayal of Clay the horseman.

In contrast stands the excellent study by Jeff Meyer in the Kentucky Historical Society journal.[345] Meyer examines not only Henry Clay's activity but also that of his family for two more generations to describe the Clay legacy. Meyer notes that eleven Kentucky Derby winners can trace their lineage to Henry Clay horses, even though the first Kentucky Derby was not run until almost a quarter century after Clay's death.[346]

Henry Clay purchased his first stallion in 1806 and was entering his horses in thoroughbred races by at least three years later if not sooner. He established his breeding and training program at his Ashland estate, located just outside Lexington on the east—at its largest, it was more than six hundred acres. It lay between the road to Richmond and one of the roads leading to the Kentucky River opposite a small waterway called Tates Creek. At the time, all major roads outside the Lexington city limits were owned and operated by private toll road companies, and tollbooths were erected every five miles. Clay's farm had tollbooths along each of the boundaries, but it also extended inside the locations of the toll gates such that he could go to and from town without incurring a charge. For those familiar with Lexington, the innermost boundary was about present-day Rose Street at the very western edge of Clay's Lexington, and the outer limits extended along Tates Creek Road to Lakeshore Drive, thence along Lakeshore and around in a northerly line inside Lake Ellerslie to Richmond Road.

As much as Clay loved his public life in politics and government, he loved his retreats, some voluntary, some forced, to Ashland, writing that he was "getting a passion for rural occupations; and feel more and more as if I ought to abandon forever the strife of politics. I would not be unhappy if a sense of public duty shall leave me free to pursue my present inclinations."[347]

The story of Henry Clay's first stallion is interesting not only for the horse itself but also for an innovation by Clay and his partners in the horse. The horse, called *Buzzard*, was purchased by Clay and four other men for the "extraordinary price" of $5,500 in 1806.[348]

The practice at the time was for the purchaser of a stallion to do so for the purpose of breeding only to his own mares. This may have been their original intent, but by 1808, Clay and his partners had, in essence, invented the modern stallion syndicate by owning the horse jointly and were advertising *Buzzard* to stand at stud for a forty-dollar fee.[349] Equine law attorney Richard Vimont described this syndicate and the horse in a speech at the Kentucky Horse Park on the opening of a special exhibit of Clay horses in 2005.[350]

Buzzard was bred in England and had a very successful racing career there, winning thirty-four races between 1792 and 1794.[351] After he was retired to stud, his progeny won more than one hundred races in England between 1799 and 1805; the next year, a *Buzzard* filly won the Oaks Stakes, the greatest of the races for fillies in England. In the early 1800s, he was purchased by Colonel John Hoomes, a Virginia breeder, and brought to stand at his stud farm in Bowling Green, Virginia. Following the breeder's death in 1806, his estate put the stallion up for sale.

Buzzard. Photograph courtesy of Ashland, the Henry Clay Estate.

Meyer calculates that the $5,500 sale price would be worth about $67,000 in 2003, which sounds low for a well-performing stallion in today's prices; but it should be known that the horse was blind in one eye, had a dislocated hip and had to be walked through the mountains from Virginia to Lexington at the age of somewhere around nineteen.[352]

Within a year of arrival in Lexington, Clay and his partners devised the syndicate format of the stallion owners having the right to breed their own mares and also share in the breeding fees payed by other mare owners. For those familiar with breeding agreements today, a fee can be either on a "live foal" or not basis, with the fee for the former generally being higher, as it involves the right to a successive breeding if a live foal does not survive. In the Clay syndicate, according to Vimont, the breeding was on a "no live foal" basis, but the mare owner, if he still owned the same mare a year later, could have a second attempt.

Buzzard's career as a stud in Kentucky ended with his death after two years; but the syndicate model designed by Clay and his partners was used in the thoroughbred industry for more than one hundred years.[353]

The follow-up question, of course, is how well did the *Buzzard* offspring lines do? As noted earlier, Ashland only follows mare bloodlines, and two of Clay's major mares will be discussed shortly. But the Pedigree Online Thoroughbred Database follows both sire and mare lines. Based thereon, *every one* of the horses running in the 2017 Kentucky Derby, including eventual Triple Crown winner *Justify*, can claim linage from *Buzzard*. It does take eighteen to nineteen generations (depending on age at breeding, etc.) to reach all the way back, but each of the horses was a *Buzzard* progeny. Further, each horse's pedigree traces to either *Mr. Prospector* (bred 1970) or *Native Dancer* (bred 1961) or both, and both of those sires are descendant from *Buzzard*.

Henry Clay began racing his horses in 1809 and at least by 1810 was racing his *Buzzard* progeny. He joined the Lexington Jockey Club in 1809 and campaigned his horses at the Jockey Club Williams Track. By 1830, he had formally established his Ashland Thoroughbred Stock Farm and began an aggressive program of acquiring additional stock, frequently with partners, and breeding to improve his lines. He began his own stud book and recorded the stallions and mares, their foals and racing records.[354]

In 1845, three horses arrived at Ashland Stud as political gifts to Clay: *Margaret Wood*, *Magnolia* and *Yorktown*. These three are generally credited with establishing the "extraordinary success" of Clay's breeding program and produced at least twelve Kentucky Derby winners.[355] Three of the runners

Photograph showing the trees (*bottom center*) outlining the former Henry Clay training track. *Lexington History Museum, Inc.*

in the 2017 Kentucky Derby trace their lines back to *Margaret Wood* and *Magnolia*: *Girvin, Hence* and *Classic Empire*.[356]

To give some context to these political gifts, Clay had just lost his 1844 race for president the prior year.[357]

Margaret Wood would be a successful horse for Clay on the track and in breeding. She is in the pedigree of four nineteenth-century Kentucky Derby winners.

Magnolia became one of the most successful broodmares in the country. All thirteen of her foals were winners, and one of them, *Kentucky*, was thought to be the best racehorse ever foaled in America. Her nickname was "The Empress of the Stud Book."[358] Henry Clay's son John took over the thoroughbred operations, and the last foal he bred from *Magnolia* was *Victory* by *Uncle Vic*, son of the famous *Lexington*. John Clay raced the horse lightly over the next several years and in 1873 George Armstrong Custer purchased *Victory* as one of his mounts. Custer was riding *Victory* on the day of the Battle of the Little Bighorn. The horse's fate is unknown.[359]

After Clay's death in 1852, John continued his operations at "Ashland-on-Tates Creek Farm," while brother James purchased Clay's house and about half of the farm. He rebuilt the house and, after a trip to New York, became interested in trotting horses. He purchased *Mambrino Chief* for the high price of $4,000 and brought him to Kentucky. He laid out a mile track on his portion of his father's farm, along the Richmond Road, and started the process of introducing harness racing to Kentucky in 1854. John innovated breeding thoroughbreds to trotters, earning a reputation for scientific practices and for establishing a new breed, the standardbred.[360]

Following James Clay's death in 1864, his widow sold the estate in 1866, and for fourteen years it was the campus of Kentucky A&M, the early name for the present University of Kentucky. The college relocated to its Euclid Avenue campus in 1879, and the farm was leased out.[361]

Finally, in 1882, Henry Clay McDowell and his wife, Anne, daughter of Henry Clay Jr., purchased Ashland and began restoring the house and grounds to a working equine operation again, possibly building a third racetrack on the property. He was already an established standardbred breeder and a fan of coaching.

FORGOTTEN FARMS

A direct consequence of municipal growth is that farmland becomes city land. When a significant portion of that growth is occasioned by people moving into the community, many don't know or even stop to think that their house or apartment or condo might be in what was once the infield of a racetrack or the pasture of a horse farm. This chapter looks, in no particular order, at a few of the former horse farms now in the city of Lexington, Kentucky, or, more accurately, the Lexington-Fayette Urban County Government.

MEADOWTHORPE STUD

Meadowthorpe subdivision is located on the Leestown Pike west of downtown Lexington. A farm of long standing, it was sold in 1886 to William H. Cheppu, whom the *Lexington Transcript* identified as a well-known bookmaker during the era when bookmaking was an acknowledged occupation. However, Cheppu was not ultimately successful in his calling, and an "overdraft" of $32,000 forced him to sell his 222-acre farm in 1892. The purchaser was Colonel James E. Pepper, owner of the Pepper bourbon distillery on Manchester Street, which he founded in 1869. The area is currently experiencing a commercial revival known as the Distillery District. Subdivision of the farm into residential lots began in 1949 and now consists of 498 properties.[362] Pepper has been described as "one of

Kentucky Whiskey's first families" and a famous thoroughbred breeder in his time who established Meadowthorpe Stables and Meadowthorpe Stud on the property.[363]

This former thoroughbred farm has one more distinction, however, between its use as a horse farm and its conversion into residential use: it was Lexington's first municipal airport. It was known as Halley's Field after then owner Dr. Samuel Halley, and airplanes began landing there as early as 1921, with the city airport officially opened May 28, 1927. The famous aviator Charles Lindbergh landed there on March 28, 1928. Halley Field hosted air circuses, air shows, flight training lessons and served several small airlines. The property reverted to farmland in 1934.[364]

Halley Field quickly became obsolete as large airplanes, multiple-engine craft and runway restrictions came about. The Airport Committee of the Board of Commerce leased Glengarry Farm, later known as Cool Meadow Farm, on the Newtown Pike for a new airport in 1930. It served the community for about twenty-five years until the current Bluegrass Field was built in the 1950s across from Keeneland Race Course. Cool Meadow today is home to the Fasig Tipton Company.

BELL PLACE

Across the Richmond Road from the western portion of Henry Clay's Ashland was Bell Place, which around 1900 was owned by the third generation of the Bell family. The farm featured dense woods except for about an acre immediately around the ornate main house. As with other former farms, particularly one barely outside the city limits, this is now an established residential area. However, the main house and grounds are now owned by the municipal government. The carriage house and stable are now home to a community theater.[365]

MERRICK PLACE

Merrick Place, the horse farm, was established before the Civil War on Tates Creek Pike.[366] The manor house was extensively remodeled by Cal Milam in 1836. Milan trained *Exterminator*, who won the 1918 Kentucky Derby,

Merrick Inn. *Photograph by author.*

as well as *Tut Tut*, who won every race he entered in 1920 as a two-year-old thoroughbred, and several other successful horses. Milam's most famous horse, however, was *Merrick*, bred in 1903. He won 62 races in his career and overall finished in the money 157 times. When the horse died in 1941 at the age of thirty-eight, he was the oldest thoroughbred on record. *Merrick* is buried in the grassy circle in front of the Merrick Inn.

Currently, the former farm is the location of a large apartment complex. The manor house has been home to the Merrick Inn, one of Lexington's premier restaurants, for more than forty years.[367]

KIRKLEVINGTON

On the other side of Tates Creek Pike and slightly farther from town from Merrick Place was the five-hundred-acre training and breeding farm of Kirklevington. It has been described as a "superbly located, well watered" estate with "sloping hillsides, picturesque lowlands and unmolested woods." In the early 1900s, it was owned by Archie L. Hamilton, who, while maintaining his own stable, focused on breeding and training thoroughbreds owned by wealthy out-of-state clients.[368]

PENMOKEN FARM

Along the present South Limestone/Nicholasville Road corridor, lying on the west side between present Southland Drive and Rosemont Garden, was the Penmoken Farm. It was about two hundred acres in size and, in contrast to other farms mentioned, had a large herd of Shetland ponies. It is also a residential subdivision.[369]

INGLESIDE FARM

Described in 1903 as being "almost at the gates of Lexington," Ingleside Farm was on the road to Harrodsburg now called South Broadway. The family of Colonel Hart Gibson bred both thoroughbred and standardbreds at the turn of the past century. The prominent feature of the entrance was a two-story "porter's house" in the middle of which was an arched gateway into the farm, topped with what appear to be castle-like battlements. While

Ingelside Farm (former) gatehouse, 2018. *Photograph by author.*

Ingelside Farm gatehouse, circa 1900. *Country Estates of the Bluegrass.*

the farm has been developed, the porter's house remains, the archway filled in and the whole repurposed for offices. Were it not for the battlements, it would not be recognizable.[370]

SPRINGHURST FARM

The Springhurst Farm was on the east side of Harrodsburg Road, farther out from Ingleside, being about 160 acres opposite the present Turfland Mall. During the 1800s, it was a premier thoroughbred breeding operation under the Pattersons. In 1893, Charles Railey purchased the property and converted it into a saddlehorse breeding and training farm and for several years showed championship horses. A spring on the property was reputed to have been the site of a "pitched battle" between certain Indian tribes. Today, it is residential and can be located by the fact its central street is named for the farm.[371]

Beaumont Farm

Beaumont Farm contained more than eight hundred acres and was a well-established thoroughbred breeding farm by 1900. Operated at that time by Hal Price Headley, it had a deserved reputation for fast horses and beautiful pastures, paddocks and farm buildings.[372] Beaumont subdivision today has primarily business and commercial areas along Harrodsburg Road, blending into a mix of townhouses and apartments on into single family residences.

McGrathiana Farm

McGrathiana Farm was located on the Newtown Pike north of Lexington and contained more than twenty-two hundred acres. Thoroughbred horses bred there by Colonel Milton Young won "fame and fortune" for their owners on racetracks in the United States and Europe.[373] The name comes from Price McGrath, who once owned it. Today, it is an office and research park owned by the University of Kentucky.

Loudoun Farm

Loudoun Farm was situated northeast of Lexington a century ago, with stands of trees dating to the colonial period and before. The curtilege is dominated by an imposing, castle-like house. One owner, Colonel William Cassius Goodloe, served as the United States minister to Brussels, and he brought back from Europe hand-carved furniture with which he populated the grand drawing room.[374] Today, the land around the farm is residential and Loudoun House is owned by the Lexington government and serves as headquarters for the Lexington Art League.

Gainesway Farm

In 1944, Clarence F. Gaines bought 280 acres on the Tates Creek Road, where he located his standardbred horse-breeding operation, which he had started in 1925. He averaged about forty-two mares and bred mostly to his own stallions.[375] Upon his death, his son John Gaines took over the business and farm; however, his plan relied more on the stallion side of the business, and John increased the number of studs and reduced significantly the number of mares.[376] In 1957, John sold the farm to a development company of which he was a co-owner in what was described at the time as "the largest land purchase for home building purposes in Central Kentucky." By then, the farm had increased in size to more than 300 acres. The intent was to create a "country club" style estate with the houses surrounding a clubhouse with tennis courts, a swimming pool, a baseball field and a stocked fishing pond. Two barns were to be retained for the use of the owners as stables, and bridle paths were to lead through the property.[377]

Entrance to Gainesway subdivision. *Photograph by author.*

The resulting development, however, was at odds with the original concept. A large space in the middle area became the campus for the Tates Creek public elementary, middle and senior high schools, and a significant portion became a public golf course, although it does have a pool.

PATCHEN WILKES FARM

Patchen Wilkes Farm is located on the Winchester Road east of Lexington. In 1900, it contained several thousand acres and was a trotting-horse operation with large barns for colts and mares, a training barn and its own training track. Many notable standardbred horses were bred, raised and trained on the farm, and at one time four notable stallions, including namesake *Patchen Wilkes*, were standing at stud.[378] Current owner Warren Rosenthal changed the farm to a thoroughbred farm when he acquired it and is presently developing the portions along Winchester Road into upscale residential houses. The farm itself is bordered on three sides by developed areas and on the fourth by an interstate.

HAMBURG PLACE

Across Winchester Road from Patchen Wilkes and likewise bordered by developed land and an interstate is Hamburg Place. John E. Madden, famously the "Wizard of the Turf," sold the horse *Hamburg* in 1897 for more than $40,000, setting a record price at the time for a horse in training. He used $30,000 of the proceeds to purchase a 235-acre farm then known as Overton Place. Henry Clay is said to have been married in the main house on the farm.[379] By 1903, the farm had been expanded by Madden to 1,600 acres.[380] Just a few years later, the farm reached its ultimate size of 2,000 acres.

Madden changed the name of the farm to Hamburg Place in honor of the horse that provided the initial funds to purchase it, and he began developing his breeding and training operations. Madden, who had boxed, frequently for prize money, in his youth, built a two-story gymnasium on the farm and frequently held boxing matches.[381] In time, he ceased control, and operations passed to his sons. In 1956, grandson Preston Madden assumed control and began breeding, training and selling horses.[382] He developed a five-and-one-half-furlong training track on the property with a carefully calculated spiral easement for the turns, enabling a rider to breeze a horse for a half mile without making sharp turns. The track also had both a dirt surface on the inside and a turf surface on the outside, the weather dictating which surface was used for training.[383]

In 1964, Interstate 75 cut through Hamburg Place, leaving 1,200 acres on the "inside" or Lexington side of the highway and 700 acres on the east side. The Madden family has begun development of the property on the Lexington side with a regional shopping mall, offices and apartments and residential lot sections. Plans eventually call for the section on the east of the interstate to be developed as well.[384]

THE EARL OF DERBY GOES TO THE KENTUCKY DERBY

Those familiar with Kentucky Derby Week in Louisville know that, in addition to the hot-air balloon and steamboat races, Friday's race card features the running of the Kentucky Oaks. The Oaks is a mile-and-one-eighth race for three-year-old thoroughbred fillies. It was first run at Churchill Down on May 19, 1875. The next day is the running of the Kentucky Derby, for three-year-old thoroughbreds, regardless of sex, at one and one-quarter miles. It, too, was first run in 1875, but, interestingly, it was run two days before the Oaks, on May 17.

Their antecedents, however, run back much further in history.

It was a scene that would be familiar to central Kentucky horsemen and their friends. A party was being held on a horse farm and estate, and the guests and their host began talking about horses, in particular their horses. They lamented that there was not a good race to test their fillies. The host, however, was the Twelfth Earl of Derby, Edward Smith-Stanley, or Lord Stanley, and the year was 1778. They decided to hold a race for fillies the next year and named it The Oaks, after the name of Derby's country estate. Lord Derby's horse won.

This race continues to run and has spawned imitators around the world, including the Irish Oaks, the New Zealand Oaks, the Oaks d'Italia and, of course, the Kentucky Oaks.[385]

The event was such a success that Lord Stanley and his friends decided to run a new race the following year open to all three-year-old thoroughbreds. At the party where the new race was planned, the guests decided it should

Edward Stanley, Seventeenth Earl of Derby. *By Sir William Orpen.*

be named either for the Earl of Derby or for Sir Charles Bunbury, who was steward of the English Jockey Club. Legend has it that the decision was made by a coin toss; Lord Stanley won, thus initiating the English or Epsom Derby. Bunbury would later get a race named in his honor, the Bunbury Cup, run at Newmarket. The first running of the Epson Derby was on May 4, 1780.

This race, too, inspired other races to be similarly named, and there are derbies in Ireland, France, Germany, Italy, Australia, New Zealand and at several race courses in the United States, including the Kentucky Derby.[386]

In the early 1870s, Louisville was without a racetrack, and horsemen discussed how they could start a new track. They called on Colonel Meriwether Lewis Clark Jr., whose grandfather co-led the famous Lewis and Clark Expedition exploring the Louisiana Purchase territory. He undertook to go to Epsom in England to view the Derby and Oaks, then he went to Paris, France, where a new jockey club had been organized in 1863, to watch its great race at Longchamp. Thus informed, Clark brought what he had learned about tracks and racing, including the idea of a Kentucky Oaks and Kentucky Derby, back to Louisville. He helped organize the Louisville Jockey Club, raise money for a track and facilities and find the land, donated by brothers John and Henry Churchill. On May 17, 1875, the first Kentucky Derby was run before an estimated crowd of ten thousand spectators. And a tradition was established.[387]

The Stanley family, Earls of Derby, have played major roles in English history since at least the 1400s.

In 1485, upstart Henry Tudor of the Lancasterians was challenging King Richard III for the throne. By virtue of his second marriage, Thomas Stanley had become Henry's stepfather. Henry and Richard met in the decisive Battle of Bosworth Field. Stanley and his brother gathered their forces on a hill overlooking the two rivals and their armies but did not take sides. Finally, seeing that Henry had achieved the advantage, they entered the fray on his side. Thomas Stanley's reward from the new Henry VII was to be named the first Earl of Derby.[388]

An announcement appeared in the *Lexington Leader* 445 years later that the Seventeenth Earl of Derby, Edward George Villiers Stanley, would visit Lexington and then go to Louisville for the Kentucky Derby—so far as is known, the first time any of the Derbys came to Kentucky.[389]

This Derby followed his ancestors in military and political service in England, serving in various regiments during the 1880s as a young man (he was born on April 4, 1865), then entering Parliament in 1892. Between then and 1906, when he lost his seat in the general election of that year, he served variously as Lord of the Treasury, Financial Secretary to the War Office and Postmaster General. His father died in 1908; succeeding to the earldom, he entered the House of Lords. In April 1918, Edward became ambassador to France. He donated a silver cup to the French authorities, the Lord Derby Cup, for a rugby championship as his father, the Sixteenth Earl, had donated the Stanley Cup for hockey.[390]

Throughout his career, Lord Stanley maintained a keen interest in thoroughbreds and his own racing stables. He was leading owner seven times during his lifetime and leading breeder ten times. His horses won the Epson Derby six times between 1924 and 1942.[391] Upon his death, the *Bloodstock Breeders Review*, considered an authoritative source, said: "Throughout the long history of the British Thoroughbred no single breeder exercised more influence on the breed than the late earl."[392]

Lord Stanley, Earl of Derby, was not making his visit as a publicity stunt. He was a breeder and owner of fame on his own and would have been welcomed as such by the Kentucky racing community. Five days after the announcement, the newspaper ran an extensive report of the breeding and racing success of the earl, noting his political and military achievements as well as those on the track, including that his horse had won the Epsom Oaks four times. It noted that the earl, sixty-six years old at the time of his visit, currently stood the leading English sire at his estate. He was not without his Lexington connections. One horse bred by Stanley was at Hal Price Headley's Beaumont Farm, and the earl himself had leased another to his host, Joseph E. Widener, owner of Elmendorf Farm on Paris Pike north of Lexington.[393]

Widner made his fortune in the traction business in Philadelphia.[394] At its peak under James Ben Ali Haggin, Elmendorf Farm comprised more than 8,500 acres, almost all in Fayette County (Lexington).[395] In about 1906, the Louisville & Nashville Railroad constructed a one-mile spur track into the farm, which was later connected at the farm's Paris Pike entrance to the interurban rail system, which ran out from Lexington to surrounding communities.[396]

The earl's trip began in New York, where his ship, the *Aquitania*, docked after crossing the Atlantic. He was met there by Widener. From there, the earl and his company would travel to Washington, D.C., to meet President Herbert Hoover. They would then travel to Lexington.[397] The visits were described by the *Lexington Leader* as a "round of social entertainment in New York and Washington."

The *Aquitania*, "The Ship Beautiful," was a Cunard Line vessel introduced in 1914 with the intent that it be the most opulent ship afloat. It was launched on April 21, 1913, by the Countess of Derby as the largest ocean liner in Great Britain. Following the sinking of the *Titanic* the year before, plans had been revised to make the *Aquitania* safer and more watertight.[398] The Earl of Derby would later return to England aboard its sister ship the *Mauretania*, "The Grand Old Lady of the Atlantic." Cunard's third sister ship in this series was the *Lusitania*, which was sunk by the German navy on May 7, 1915.[399]

The earl arrived in Lexington in Widener's private railway car on the morning of May 14 at the Southern Railway station on South Broadway. They announced he would visit a half dozen or more famous central Kentucky horse farms over the next two days. Social engagements would include dinners and luncheons at various farms. The news reports do not say, but it is likely for both ease and security that the earl and his host took the private car over the tracks to Elmendorf Farm's spur and thence to the residence.[400]

To cap off matters, for the first time in the history of the Kentucky Derby, the governor, Flem D. Sampson, declared Derby Day a state holiday in honor of Lord Stanley's visit![401]

However, from the standpoint of the social scene, calamity struck. The Earl of Derby had come down with a cold and was cancelling engagements, at first just for Thursday. By the next day, his cancellations extended to include all local events, a dinner in Louisville and a Derby morning breakfast. As it happened, Rear Admiral Cary T. Grayson, former personal physician to President Woodrow Wilson, was in Lexington for the races and was called to Elmendorf to examine the earl. Said to be running a slight fever, he was advised to take bed rest and call off his engagements. However, the paper reported, "his lordship was quite sure, however, that his indisposition will sufficiently improve" to permit him to attend the Kentucky Derby.[402]

The previous day, the newspaper had reported that a dispatch from Liverpool, England, near the ancestral estate of the Earls of Derby, stated that the country estate, in the family for five centuries, had been placed for sale on the market due to increases in taxation and duties. The estate comprised 2,500 acres. The Earl's secretary, traveling with him, issued a denial from Elmendorf Farm. Unaddressed was whether Lord Stanley simply desired to avoid conversation over the matter and conveniently came down with his cold.[403]

His "strength regained," as predicted, the Earl of Derby, with Mr. and Mrs. Widener and Admiral Grayson, left Elmendorf at 9:30 a.m. on Derby Saturday, traveling in Widener's private car *The Lynnewood* pulled by a special train from Lexington to Louisville.[404] Along the way, a stop at the station in Frankfort drew a crowd of "several hundreds," and Lord Stanley addressed them from the car. He ventured the opinion that *Gallant Fox*, an entry from Woodford County, would win.[405]

The experienced horseman was correct. *Gallant Fox* with Earl Sande in the saddle came in first, which led to a series of stories with plays on words about the "two earls." Of special note is that Sande won his third Derby this day, equaling the previous record of African American and Lexington jockey Isaac Murphy.[406] The Earl of Derby had watched the first three races from a private box in the clubhouse before descending to a specially constructed "pagota" in an enclosure near the finish line to watch the Derby. Prior to the races beginning, the earl held a press conference at which he made the statement that he might race his horses in America in the future.[407]

The Earl of Derby and his party returned to New York, likely in Widener's private car, for a day of racing at Belmont, being only the second time he had ever seen racing on dirt. On May 21, 1930, Lord Stanley and his party boarded the *Mauretania* for the return voyage to England.[408]

NOTES

The History of the Horse

1. Phelps, *Notable North American Thoroughbreds*, 12.
2. International Museum of the Horse, *Hyracotherium*, http://imh.org/exhibits/online/hyracotherium-eohippus (accessed April 27, 2017). Hereinafter cited as IMH.
3. Ibid.
4. Phelps, *Notable North American Thoroughbreds*, 12.
5. IMH, http://imh.org/exhibits/online/mesohippus (accessed April 27, 2017).
6. Phelps, *Notable North American Thoroughbreds*.
7. IMH, http://imh.org/exhibits/online/pliohippus (accessed April 27, 2017).
8. Phelps, *Notable North American Thoroughbreds*; Gregory L. Ferraro, "The Corruption of Nobility," *American Eye* (May/June 1992): 4, accessed April 24, 2017, www.jstor.org/stable/25125367?seq=1#page_scaan_tab_contents.
9. Phelps, *Notable North American Thoroughbreds*.
10. Ibid.
11. Ibid., 13.
12. *Encyclopedia Britannica*, "Horse Racing," 2, accessed May 17, 2017, https://www.britannica.com/sports/horse-racing#ref9192. Hereinafter *EB*.
13. Broden, *Silks and Satins*.
14. *Wikipedia*, "Parthian shot," accessed September 21, 2017, https://en.wikipedia.org/wiki/Parthian_shot.
15. Weeks, *American Turf*, 11.
16. *EB*, "Horse Racing," 2.
17. Eventing horses are not required to be a "purebred" of one kind or another, but thoroughbreds or horses with thoroughbred ancestry dominate.

18. "About Eventing," accessed September 21, 2017, https://kentuckythreedayevent. com/about-eventing.

19. Mike Parker, "The History of Horse Racing," 1, accessed November 14, 2016, http://www.mrmike.com/Explore/hrhst.htm.

20. *EB*, "Horse Racing," 3.

21. Weeks, *American Turf*, 12.

22. Parker, "History of Horse Racing," 2.

23. Weeks, *American Turf*, 21. The English Stud Book will make a dramatic reappearance in 1913 and contribute to almost ending racing in the United States.

24. There are several horse breeds, not counting interbreeding. The American saddlebred, for example, is popular but is shown, not raced. Other breeds include the European warmbloods and even the Kentucky mountain horse. This work will focus on racing in Kentucky, which is primarily done by thoroughbreds and standardbreds.

25. The name has its origin in a set of standards or requirements of size and gait as well as breeding.

26. "The History of Trotting," accessed November 14, 2016, http://www.trotting. com/trotting-history.

Racing in Early America

27. Crews, "Gambling," 7, http://www.history.org/Foundation/journal/ Autumn08/ gamble.cfm.

28. *EB*, "Horse Racing."

29. Crews, "Gambling," 1.

30. "Colonial Horses," International Museum of the Horse, 2, accessed December 6, 2017, http://imh.org/exhibits/on-line/legacy-of-the-horse/colonial-horses.

31. Ibid.

32. Emily Davidson, "Horse Racing in the Colonies," accessed December 6, 2017, http://prezi.com/xntvtdzwi-*h/horse-racing-in-the-colonnies.

33. Breen, "Horses and Gentlemen," 239.

34. "Early History of Thoroughbred Horses in Virginia," Virginia History Series #11–08, 2008, accessed December 6, 2017, http://virginiahistoryseries.org/ linked/unit 11.early history of thoroughbred horses in virginia.allslides.pdf. Obviously, claim to the "first" conflicts with the New Amsterdam races.

35. Harold B. Gill Jr., "A Sport Only for Gentlemen," Colonial Williamsburg, accessed December 6, 2017, http://www.history.org/history/teaching/ enewsletter/volume4/march06/sport.cfm.

36. Breen, "Horses and Gentlemen," 251.

37. "Colonial Horses."

38. *Encyclopedia Britannica*, "Thoroughbred," accessed December 3, 2017, https://britannica.com/animal/Thoroughbred.

39. "Early History of Thoroughbred Horses in Virginia," Virginia History Series.

40. Gill, "A Sport Only for Gentlemen," 2–3.

41. Ambrose, *Kentucky Association*, 76.

42. Gill, "A Sport Only for Gentlemen," 1.

43. Breen, "Horses and Gentlemen," 253–254.

44. Ibid., 256.

45. Davidson, "Horse Racing in the Colonies."

46. Crews, "Gambling," 6.

47. Bill Sullivan, "Riders Up! Horse Racing in 18th-Century Williamsburg," Making History, May 6, 2016, accessed December 6, 2017, http://makinghistorynow.com/2016/05/riders-up-horse-racing-in-williamsburg.

48. "Presidents at the Races," White House Historical Association, accessed December 6, 2017, https://www.whitehousehistory.org/white-house-horses/presidents-at-the-races.

49. IMH, 4.

The Church Horses Built

50. This chapter is largely based on an article in the *Daily Racing Form* by Evan Hammonds, September 15, 1996, 21.

51. This movement and its effects on racing in Kentucky are treated in a separate chapter of this work.

52. A parish house is a secondary structure usually housing church offices and administrative areas and occasionally living quarters for a priest.

53. Wall, *How Kentucky Became Southern*, 227–228.

54. "The Episcopal Church of the Good Shepherd History," 4, accessed May 1, 2017, http://goodshepherdlex.org/History. Other information from this site is supplied herein.

55. *Daily Racing Form.*

Jockeys' Silks

56. *The Benson and Hedges Book of Racing Colors*, Jockeys' Association of Great Britain, 1973, xvii.

57. Frederick M. Borden, *Silks and Satins*, unpublished manuscript 1966, Keeneland Library, Lexington, Kentucky. Pages are unnumbered.

58. Ibid.

59. Herbert, *A History of Racing Silks*, 4–5.

60. Ibid., 6.

61. Borden, *Silks and Satins*.

62. Herbert, *A History of Racing Silks*, 7.

63. Ibid., 10–17.

64. Ibid., 28.

65. Ibid., 32.

66. Ibid., 37–38.

67. Sheena McKenzie, "Hot to Trot: The Secrets and Superstitions of Jockey Fashions," *Washington Post*, accessed September 24, 2017, http://edition.cnn.com/2013/06/10/sport/jockey-silks-jackets-horse-racing.

68. Bill Christine, *Daily Racing Form*, accessed September 24, 2017, http://www.drf.com/events/top-10-most-eclectic-silks-racing-history.

69. *Benson and Hedges*, 3.

They're Off!

70. Tom Eblen, *Lexington Herald-Leader*, "Why a Funny Looking '95 Cadillac Might Be the 'Best Place' to Watch a Horse Race," October 8, 2017, 1C. The article credits Stephen G. Phillips with inventing the mobile gate.

71. *Thoroughbred Record*, September 30, 1981, 1865.

72. Keig, *Racing Silks and Winning Colors*, 11.

73. Weeks, *American Turf*, 25.

74. *Thoroughbred Record*.

75. *Horse Racing's Top 100 Moments*, 67. Hereinafter *Top 100*.

76. Ibid.

77. "New Barriers," *Daily Examiner*, December 30, 1935.

78. *Thoroughbred Record*.

79. *Lexington Herald-Leader*, March 9, 1973.

80. *Top 100*, 68.

81. Marshall Cassidy, *Daily Racing Form*, letter to the editor, July 31, 1994.

82. *Daily Racing Form*, August 3, 1966.

83. Ibid., November 30, 1964.

Resting in Peace

84. Thoroughbred Heritage, accessed July 20, 2017, www.tbheritage.com/index.html.

85. Kleber, *Kentucky Encyclopedia*, 551.

86. Weeks, *American Turf*, 30.

87. "The Horse Named Lexington," accessed September 29, 2017, www.visitlex.com/about/blue-horse/lexington, hereinafter Visitlex.

88. Kleber, *Kentucky Encyclopedia*, 551.

89. Visitlex.

90. Kleber, *Kentucky Encyclopedia*.

91. Visitlex.

92. Kleber, *Kentucky Encyclopedia*.

93. Frances J. Karon, *Running Rough Shod*, "On Hallowed Ground: The Calumet Cemetery," 2–3, accessed September 29, 2017, http:/www.runroughshod. blogspot.com/2014/11/on-hallowed-ground-calumet-cemetery.html.

94. Hollingsworth, *Wizard of the Turf*, 83.

95. "Hamburg Place Horse Cemetery," accessed September 28, 2017, http:/www. waymarking.com/waymarks/WM2KMJ_Hamburg_Place.

96. Tom Eblen, "Farm Had Two Cemeteries," *Lexington Herald-Leader*, August 10, 2017, accessed August 10, 2017, http:/kentucky.com/news/local/news-columns-blogs/tom/eblen/article166466297.html.

McDowell Speedway

97. *Lexington Leader*, "Gala Day for Blue Grass Reinsmen," July 31, 1904, 6, col. 1. Hereinafter Reinsmen.

98. This may have been the trotting track at Mentelle Park, which was sold in 1872, to be renamed the "Ashland Driving Park." *Daily Press*, September 9, 1872, 4, col. 1. The race happened two months before the sale was reported, and the pending change in ownership may have been the reason for moving the race.

99. Dr. Herr's track lay between the Nicholasville turnpike and the railroad just outside city limits to the south. Herr Park would be developed into a residential development as the city expanded in 1893. Its streets were named for newspapers: Gazette, Transcript, Press and Leader. Today, it is part of the University of Kentucky medical complex campus. "Herr Park Subdivision," Fayette County Clerk's Office, Lexington, Kentucky.

100. *Daily Press*, September 9, 1872, 4, col. 1.

101. "Amateur Racing," *Daily Press*, July 11, 1872, 4, col. 2. The article runs two columns. It was not unusual for such extensive detailed reporting on races, not only locally but from other cities. The *Lexington Leader* for July 17, 1904, also reports on carriage races in Columbus, Ohio.

102. *Lexington Leader*, July 17, 1904, 3, col. 4. Likewise, the next column discussed the possible closure of a track in Illinois.

103. *Lexington Leader*, July 25, 1902, 2, col. 1.

104. Coleman, *Squire's Sketches of Lexington*, 72.enry

105. *Lexington Leader*, July 22, 1897, 8, col. 2.

106. Ockerman, *Historic Lexington*, 23.

107. Wendy Bright, *History of a House Museum*, "Ashland, The Henry Clay Estate," accessed October 2, 2017, http:/www.historyofahousemuseum.com/tag/major-henry-clay.

108. Wall, *How Kentucky Became Southern*, 38ff.
109. Ockerman; Ernie W. Stamper, "The Gratz of Gratz Park," 18.
110. *Lexington Herald*, April 23, 1900, 1, col. 6.
111. William M. Ambrose, "McDowell Speedway," unpublished manuscript referenced at length with permission, 2017.

America's First Professional Athlete Class

112. John Cheves, *Lexington Herald-Leader*, "Jockey Discovers History of Black Horsemen at Local Cemetery," accessed January 10, 2017, http://kentucky.com/news/local/counties/fayette-county/article44104278.html.
113. Hollingsworth, *Lexington Queen of the Bluegrass*, 150.
114. Wall, *How Kentucky Became Southern*, 37.
115. Mooney, *Race Horse Men*, 195.
116. Ibid., 165.
117. Ibid.
118. Hotaling, *Great Black Jockeys*, 211.
119. *Daily Racing Form*, April 11, 1957, 7, col. 1.
120. See the chapter on betting for a discussion of auction pool, bookmaker and pari-mutual betting.
121. Hotaling, *Great Black Jockeys*, 229ff.
122. Ibid., 239.
123. Mooney, *Race Horse Men*, 182.
124. Hotaling, *Great Black Jockeys*, 244.
125. Ibid., 246.
126. Wall, *How Kentucky Became Southern*, 128.
127. Ibid., 129–130.
128. Mooney, *Race Horse Men*, 195.
129. Hotaling, *Great Black Jockeys*, 255.
130. Robertson, *The History of Horse Racing in America*, 165.
131. Wall, 139.
132. Ibid., 140ff.
133. Hotaling, *Great Black Jockeys*, 269.
134. Mooney, *Race Horse Men*, 210.
135. Hotaling, *Great Black Jockeys*, 271.
136. Robertson, 164.
137. Black Art Depot, accessed January 10, 2017, http://blackartdepot.com/african-american-history/10-facts-about-isaac-burns-murphy.html.
138. Hotaling, *Great Black Jockeys*, 311.
139. Ibid., 313.
140. Ibid., 318.

141. Ibid., 319.

142. Mooney, *Race Horse Men*, 215.

143. Hotaling, *Great Black Jockeys*, 312.

144. Mooney, *Race Horse Men*, 216.

145. *Wikipedia*, "James Winkfield," accessed March 12, 2017, https://en.wikipedia.org/wiki/James_Winkfield.

146. Ibid.

147. Ibid., 217.

148. Hotaling, *Great Black Jockeys*, 340.

149. Ibid., 291.

150. Mooney, *Race Horse Men*, 196.

151. Hotaling, *Great Black Jockeys*, 291.

152. Peter Brackney, "The Kaintuckeean," accessed October 11, 2017, http://www.kaintuckeean.com/2011/06/walklex-soup-perkins-alley-and-last-old.html.

153. Hotaling, *Great Black Jockeys*, 295.

154. Ibid., 296.

155. Ibid., 299.

156. Editors, *Encyclopedia Britannica*, accessed October 11, 2017, https://www.britannica.com/biography/Willie-Simms.

157. Hotaling, *Great Black Jockeys*, 289.

158. Kansas Historical Society, "Álonzo Clayton," 2017, accessed October 12, 2017, www.kshs.org/kansapedia/alonzo-clayton/17739.

159. Hotaling, *Great Black Jockeys*, 291. Finishing "in the money" means first through fourth place, which are the places among which purse money is paid.

160. Tim Talbott, "Alonzo 'Lonnie' Clayton," ExploreKYHistory, accessed October 11, 2017, http:/explorekuhistory.ky.gov/items/show/315.

161. Mooney, *Race Horse Men*, 196.

162. Kansas Historical Society.

163. Talbott, "Alonzo 'Lonnie' Clayton."

164. Wall, *How Kentucky Became Southern*, 193.

165. Ibid., 281ff.

166. Hotaling, *Great Black Jockeys*, 281ff.

167. Blackford, "Black Fences," 15.

168. Jim Embry, "Honor Legendary Black Jockey, Genesis of Idea for His Memorial," *Lexington Herald-Leader*, accessed January 10, 2017, hrrp://kentucky.com/opinion/op-ed/article 42642633.html.

169. Lexington Public Library "Visitor Guide," undated.

How Good Intentions Almost Killed Racing

170. Nicholson, *Kentucky Derby*, 19.

171. Ibid., 32.

172. Samuel W. Thomas, *Churchill Downs*, Kentucky Derby Museum, 1995, 118.

173. Nicholson, *Kentucky Derby*, 19.

174. Ibid., 20.

175. *Merriam-Webster*, "auction-pool," accessed October 11, 2017, https://www.wordnik.com/words/auction-pool.

176. *Wikipedia*, "Hart-Agnew Law," accessed October 13, 2017, https://en.wikipedia.org/wiki/Hart-Agnew_Law.

177. Bolin, *Bossism and Reform in a Southern City*, 77.

178. Nicholson, *Kentucky Derby*, 29. See the chapter of betting herein for more on pari-mutual betting and machines.

179. Bolin, *Bossism and Reform in a Southern City*, 88.

180. Harison and Klotter, *New History of Kentucky*, 353.

181. Ibid., 353

182. Thomas, *Churchill Downs*, 172. The American Book Company was an association of bookmakers.

183. Bolin, *Bossism and Reform in a Southern City*, 88–91.

184. Harison and Klotter, *New History of Kentucky*, 353.

185. Thomas, *Churchill Downs*, 118.

186. Ockerman, *Historic Lexington*, 12.

187. Ambrose, *Kentucky Association*, 65.

188. Ibid., 3.

189. Nicholson, *Kentucky Derby*, 20.

190. Bolin, *Bossism and Reform in a Southern City*, 84.

191. Thomas, *Churchill Downs*, 154.

192. Ambrose, *Kentucky Association*, 56.

193. Bolin, *Bossism and Reform in a Southern City*, 84.

194. Thomas, *Churchill Downs*, 168.

195. Ambrose, *Kentucky Association*, 57.

196. Ibid., note, 59.

197. Nicholson, *Kentucky Derby*, 48.

198. National Portrait Gallery, accessed October 31, 2017, http://www.npg.org.uk/collections/search/person/mp122437/victor-albert-george-child-villiers.

199. I am indebted to horseman Preston Madden for alerting me to the Jersey Act. Madden interview, May 17, 2017.

200. *Top 100*, 124.

201. Ibid., 124–125.

202. Ibid.

203. *Encyclopaedia Britannica*, "Jersey Act," accessed May 17, 2017, https://britannica.com/event/Jersey-Act.

204. Hollingsworth, *Wizard of the Turf*, 29.

205. Ibid., 103.

206. Ibid. Hamburg Place has been mostly developed by 2017 into a regional mall and mixed residential, business and commercial uses. Every street in the development is named for a Hamburg Place horse, including major streets Sir Barton Way and Star Shoot Parkway.
207. Ibid., 102.
208. *Top 100*, 125.

Civil War Racing in Lexington

209. All Southern tracks closed when war was declared, and almost all horses were put to war uses, either for cavalry mounts or to pull cannon and wagons.
210. Ambrose, *Kentucky Association*, 18.
211. "Racing Calendars—1861, 1862, 1863, 1864, 1865," compiled by H.G. Crickmore, privately printed by W.C. Whitney, New York, Keeneland Association Library, supplied to the author by William M. Ambrose.
212. Hollingsworth, *Lexington Queen of the Bluegrass*, 71–72.
213. "Racing Calendars"
214. National Register of Historic Places, "The Civil War in Lexington," accessed July 5, 2017, .https://nps.gov/nr/travel/lexington/civilwar.htm.
215. Ambrose, *Kentucky Association*, 19.
216. "Racing Calendars."
217. Hollingsworth, *Lexington: Queen of the Bluegrass*, 77.
218. Ambrose, *Kentucky Association*, 19.
219. Ibid., 19–20.
220. Weeks, *American Turf*, 162.
221. Ambrose, *Kentucky Association*.

Kentucky *Just* Owns *the Triple Crown*

222. Clark was the grandson of General William Clark of the Lewis and Clark Expedition, which explored the Louisiana Purchase Territory for President Thomas Jefferson. Accessed November 7, 2017, https://en.wikipedia.org/wiki/Meriwether_Lewis_Clark_Jr.
223. Harison and Klotter, *New History of Kentucky*, 188.
224. Churchill Downs, "The World's Most Legendary Racetrack," accessed November 7, 2017, www.churchilldowns.com/about/churchill-downs.
225. Klotter, *New History of Kentucky*, 189.
226. Marion E. Altieri, "The Woodlawn Vase," accessed July 11, 2017, equineinfoexchange.com.
227. Tim Talbott, "Woodlawn Race Course," accessed July 9, 2017, http://explorekyhistory.ky.gov/items/show/329.

228. "City of Woodlawn Park," accessed July 9, 2017, http://woodlawnpark.com/index.php/city-information/woodlawn-park-html.

229. Altieri, "Woodlawn Vase."

230. Marvin Drager, "August Belmont," accessed November 7, 2017, https://britannica.com/biography/August-Belmont.

231. J. Keeler Johnson, "What's in a (Race) Name?" The Sport, accessed November 7, 2017, https://www.americasbestracing.net/the-sport/2017-whats-race-name-race-and-track-august-belmont.

232. Wall, *How Kentucky Became Southern*, 170.

233. Hollingsworth, *Lexington: Queen of the Bluegrass*, 158.

234. He seems not to have preferred either "II" or "Jr.," but most sources use the Roman numerals.

235. Johnson, "What's in a (Race) Name?"

236. *Top 100*, 106.

$2 to Win on No. 5

237. Weeks, *American Turf*, 25.

238. Ambrose, *Kentucky Association*, Appendix E, 76–81.

239. *Merriam-Webster Dictionary*, "Bet," accessed November 8, 2017, http://unabridged.merriam-webster.com/unabridged/bet.

240. *Merriam-Webster Dictionary*, "Wager," accessed November 8, 2017, http://unabridged.merriam-webster.com/unabridged/wager.

241. Early wagers were only win bets; it took the development of sophisticated machines to allow place and show betting.

242. *Merriam-Webster Dictionary*, "Game," accessed November 8, 2017, http://unabridged.merriam-webster.com/unabridged/game.

243. Ambrose, *Kentucky Association*.

244. Kentucky Constitution, Section 226 (1891). Amendments in 1988 and 1992 to this section permitted a state-run lottery in conjunction with other states, and gambling, lotteries, etc., for charitable purposes. Otherwise, the prohibition on "lotteries and gift enterprises" remains in place.

245. *Encyclopedia Britannica*, "Bookmaking," accessed May 17, 2017, https://www.britannica.com/topic/bookmaking-gambling.

246. Ambrose, *Kentucky Association*, 29.

247. Vosburgh, *Racing in America*, 1922.

248. Marjorie Rieser, "Horse Racing in Central Kentucky and Jefferson County," master's thesis, 1944, 114, *Electronic Thesis and Dissertations*, Paper 2115, accessed November 16, 2017, https://doi.org/10.18297/etd/2115.

249. Tom Eblen, "Raising Money to Restore Floral Hall, Lexington's 'Round Barn,'" October 2, 2012, accessed November 14, 2017, http://tomeblen.bloginky.com/

tag/floral-hall. After the renovations described in the article, it was renamed "The Standardbred Stable of Memories" and now houses horse artifacts and archives, in addition to being rentable for events.

250. Ockerman, *Historic Lexington*, map, 31.

251. Ambrose, *Kentucky Association*, 32.

252. Weeks, *American Turf*, 423–426.

253. Raymond W. Kanzler, "When Bookies Were 'Gentlemen,'" *Baltimore Sun*, May 4, 1958, magazine section, 2.

254. *Wikipedia*, "Parimutuel Betting," accesssed July 21, 2017, https://en.wikipedia.org/wiki/Parimutuel_betting.

255. *Encyclopedia Britannica*, "Pari-mutuel," accessed May 17, 2017, https://www.britannica.com/topic/pari-mutuel.

256. Vosburgh, *Racing in America*, 56.

257. Kristina Panos, "Tote Boards: The Impressive Engineering of Horse Gambling," accessed November 7, 2017, https://hackaday.com/2015/11/04/tote-boards-the-impressive-engeering-of-horse-racing-gambling.

258. AmTote, "Company History," accessed November 7, 2017, http://www.amtote.com/company-history.

259. Panos, "Tote Boards." The complete article includes mechanical drawings illustrating the wires, pulls, gears and number wheels.

260. AmTote.

My Old Kentucky Track

261. Cathy Schenck, Keeneland librarian, list compiled from *American Turf Register*, Keeneland Library, circa 1980.

262. David Louis Thornton III, unpublished manuscript, 1965, Keeneland Library, Lexington, Kentucky, 3.

263. Ibid., 19.

264. Kentucky Historical Society, Historic Markers Database for No. 6, accessed November 21, 2017, http://migration.kentucky.gov/kyhs/hmdb/MarkerSearch.aspx?mode=All.

265. Perrin, *History of Fayette County*, 1882, 279.

266. *Keeneland Magazine* (Fall/Winter 1991): 69.

267. *Lexington Herald-Leader*, October 23, 1993.

268. Byron Crawford, *(Louisville) Courier-Journal*, June 19, 1981

269. National Register of Historic Places, Robert Sanders House nomination form, 3.

270. *(Lexington) Reporter*, August 9, 1815, 6, col. 6.

271. Tim Talbott, "Race Track, 1924–1928 (Raceland)," accessed September 24, 2017, http://explorekyhistory.ky.gov/items/show/326. Jack Keene was a noted

breeder and trainer and owned Keeneland Stud in Lexington, which would later become Keeneland Race Track.

272. Ibid.

273. Terry L. Hapney Jr., "Raceland Steep in History Thanks to Racetrack Heritage," *Greenup Beacon*, September 19, 2017, accessed September 24, 2017, http://greenupbeacon.com/raceland_racetrack.

274. Schenk, list compiled from *American Turf Register*.

275. Gary A. O'Dell, "At the Starting Post: Racing Venues and the Origins of Thoroughbred Racing in Kentucky: 1783–1865," *Register of the Kentucky Historical Society* 116, no. 1 (Winter 2018): 67.

276. Thornton, 22.

277. Ambrose, *Kentucky Association*, 1.

278. Marjorie Risner, "Horse Racing in Central Kentucky and Jefferson County," 1944, *Electronic Theses and Dissertations*, Paper 2115, 9, accessed November 16, 2017, https://doi.org/10.18297/etd2115. While Risner states the "main street of the town served as the race course," that is not clear from the newspaper advertisement announcing the race. From the detailed rules and conditions, it is clear the Lexington Jockey Club was conducting the race, but where is not stated.

279. *Minute Book of the Lexington Trustees*, 9.

280. Ibid., 32.

281. Ibid., 47–48.

282. *Lexington Gazette*, March 21, 1795, 2, col. 4.

283. Thornton, 25. Thornton reports the Kentucky General Assembly was still passing laws against horse races in public streets as late as 1821.

284. Ibid.

285. Ibid., 23.

286. Fayette County (Lexington) Clerk's Office records.

287. Randolph Hollingsworth, "She Used Her Power Lightly: A Political History of Margaret Wickliffe Preston of Kentucky," unpublished dissertation, University of Kentucky, 1999, 303–304.

288. Risner, "Horse Racing in Central Kentucky," 12. Risner describes the area as beginning at the northwest corner of today's Jefferson Street and Main Street and running back to the vicinity of Third Street. However, the cemetery property is three blocks and a line of railroad tracks farther west. She bases her location of the Jockey Club track based on correspondence of Charles R. Staples, a Lexington historian in the early 1900s. However, the area described as west of Jefferson from Main to Third is where the Todd Race Land would have been. Either Staples remembered the wrong track or Risner, not from Lexington, misinterpreted the descriptions in his letters.

289. Ambrose, *Kentucky Association*, 2; Risner, "Horse Racing in Central Kentucky," 12.

290. See, e.g., Risner, "Horse Racing in Central Kentucky," 15, for a *Kentucky Gazette* advertisement announcing that "there would be a Purse run for over the Lexington Course," 15.

291. "Lexington Races," *Kentucky Gazette*, October 10, 1795, 3, col. 3.

292. Ambrose, *Kentucky Association*, 1.

293. Lee Sollow, "Horse Owners in Kentucky in 1800," *Journal*, Kentucky Historical Society 79, no. 3 (Summer 1981): 204–205.

294. *Kentucky Reporter*, September 25, 1813, 4, col. 2.

295. O'Dell, "At the Starting Post," 20.

296. Ambrose, *Kentucky Association*, 66.

297. Hollingsworth, "She Used Her Power Lightly," 37.

298. Coleman, *Squire's Sketches of Lexington*, 30.

299. Simpson, *Bluegrass Houses and Their Traditions*, 383.

300. Ibid., 2.

301. Ibid., 6–9.

302. Ibid., 8.

303. Fayette County Deed Book 4, 181.

304. Ambrose, *Kentucky Association*, 11.

305. Coleman, *Squire's Sketches of Lexington*, 44. The area is now part of the University of Kentucky campus.

306. O'Dell, "At the Starting Post," 76.

307. Ockerman, *Historic Lexington*, 31.

308. Until the mid-1990s, the roads outside the city limits were owned by private road companies, which acquired franchises to build roads and charge tolls in return. Ibid., 32.

309. W.R. Wallis, "Map: Fayette County," Kentucky Room, Lexington Public Library, Lexington, Kentucky, map drawer 1.

310. *(Lexington) Leader*, "Trotting Industry," April 4, 1908, 2, col. 1.

311. Ibid., "Death of Dr. Herr," May 29, 1891, 8, col. 5.

312. The earliest mention in the Lexington newspapers of trotting races on the Herr Track found is the *(Lexington) Observer and Reporter*, November 11, 1866, 3, col. 4.

313. *(Lexington) Daily Press*, "Amateur Racing," July 11, 1872, 4, col 2.

314. Ibid., "Trotting Races Yesterday," August 1, 1872, 4, col.1.

315. *Lexington Transcript*, December 30, 1884, 3, col.3.

316. *Leader*, "Orloff Brought In," July 16, 1891, 8, col. 3, and "Forest Park Sold," July 15, 1891, 5, col. 3.

317. W.R. Wallis, CE, Map of Fayette County, 1891, Lexington Public Library, Kentucky Room, map drawer one. The map describes the point as a "toll gate," suggesting that it may not have been a house or a building.

318. The application is by Maprika, LLC, found at www.maprika.com. On December 6, 2017, the author used his cellphone to access the Wallis Map on the app and track down the physical location of the toll booth. The app gives credit

for "historical positioning" to Scott Clark. Maprika version 2.7.3 was used on an iPhone 9.3. The map is further identified as Map #2799. No date of creation or uploading is given.

319. "Herr Park Subdivision."

320. Ockerman, *Historic Lexington*, 34.

321. "Early Louisville Racing and Edward Troye," June 24, 2012, accessed November 14, 2016, https://kentuckyonlinearts.wordpress.com/tag/oakland-house-and-race-course.

322. Risner, "Horse Racing in Central Kentucky," 24. Risner notes that early racing in Louisville is not as well documented as in Lexington, because the community did not have early newspapers to record races and locations.

323. "Early Louisville Racing"

324. "Shippingport Island," accessed November 14, 2016, http://historiclouisville.weebly.com/shippingport-island.html.

325. Ibid.

326. Ibid. This site contains several images and photographs, including a representation of what the area would have looked like without the extensive canal enlargement and other facilities.

327. Risner, "Horse Racing in Central Kentucky," 25–29.

328. "Early Louisville Racing." An image of an 1840 painting showing the mansion that served as the clubhouse and the gathering crowd can be found on the website.

329. Ibid.

330. Risner, "Horse Racing in Central Kentucky," 32.

331. "Early Louisville Racing."

332. Peter Morrin, "Patriotism in a Bottle," *Courier Journal*, July 3, 2005, H1.

333. Vosburgh, *Racing in America*, 55.

334. Tim Talbot, "Woodlawn Race Course," ExploreKYHistory, accessed November 14, 2016, http://explorekyhistory.ky.gov/itens/show 329.

335. John C. Sheer, "Woodlawn Race Track: It's History," accessed November 14, 2016, http://neighborhoodlink.com/Beechmont/pages/49908.

336. Ibid.

337. Risner, "Horse Racing in Central Kentucky," 34. Churchill Downs was established in 1875, but as it is an active track, it is outside the scope of this work.

338. Talbott, "Douglas Park Racetrack," ExploreKYHistory, accessed November 14, 2016, http://explorehistory.ky.gov/items/show/320.

339. "Louisville Tracks," *Courier Journal*, July 21, 1977.

340. Talbott, "Douglas Park Racetrack."

Henry Clay, Horse Breeder and Racer

341. Heidler and Heidler, *Henry Clay*, 42.

342. The book runs to almost eight hundred pages of text.

343. Remini, *Henry Clay*, 804.

344. Rimini, 205. The Clay racetrack was a training track and not a place for public races except for a brief period in the early 1820s between the end of racing on the Williams Track and the beginning of racing at the Kentucky Association Track. That track, as shown by the accompanying photograph, paralleled Tates Creek Road/High Street. The starting post was probably near the turn at the top right turn of the track, as the stables and Clay's spring were in that area. If so, the back stretch ran behind the present-day Cassidy Elementary School and Morton Middle School, turning back for a home stretch in the Romany Road area.

345. Jeff Meyer, "Henry Clay's Legacy to Horse Breeding and Racing," *Register of the Kentucky Historical Society* 100, no. 4 (Autumn 2002): 473. Meyer is a former curator and registrar at Ashland, the Henry Clay Estate in Lexington, Kentucky. Meyer laments the absence of scholarly book-length studies of the Kentucky horse industry and history, which has not abated, 474, n. 2. For this reason, Meyer's article is the primary source for the rest of this review of Henry Clay's equine activity except as noted.

346. Meyer, "Henry Clay's Legacy," 473. Ashland only tracks bloodlines through Clay's mares in reaching this number. A different view from tracing the descending lines from Clay's stallion *Buzzard* is discussed later.

347. Ibid., 476, quoting from an 1830 letter to his brother-in-law, James. Brown. This was written about a year and a half after Jackson had replaced John Quincy Adams in the White House, thus ending Clay's tenure as Adams's secretary of state. The year 1829 was one of turmoil for Clay, as he returned to Lexington to restart his law practice and see to the farm. In addition, his son Thomas was arrested and jailed for nonpayment of a debt, and his stepfather, mother and older brother John all died. One cannot wonder why Clay was tempted to retire to Ashland and be a country gentleman. He did not give into this temptation and, by November 1831, was elected to the United States Senate. Remini, *Henry Clay*, xix–xx.

348. Remini, *Henry Clay*, 205, n. 40.

349. Meyer, "Henry Clay's Legacy," 477.

350. Richard Vimont, equine law attorney. Mr. Vimont has practiced law in the equine area for many years and is very familiar with equine syndication agreements. He shared his original notes for his speech; the following discussion is derived from those notes.

351. For context, Kentucky became a state on June 1, 1792.

352. The medical conditions are from Vimont, notes 2. The age is assumed based on *Buzzard* first racing as a three-year-old in 1792.

353. The model was updated in the 1930s by Leslie Combs of Spendthrift Farm outside Lexington. He increased the number of investors and the number of mares covered by a stallion in a breeding season. Some people in the industry,

including John Gaines, became concerned that the Combs-style agreement began to resemble an investment contract and the promotional material might be considered an offering of a security, which, if so determined, would bring the breeding industry under Securities and Exchange Commission regulation. Gaines submitted his "typical" stallion syndication agreement to the SEC and requested a "no action" letter, which basically would say that, based on the facts and opinions presented by the Gaines legal team, the SEC would not take any action against the participating horsemen. He obtained the desired letter. Vimont, 4–6.

354. Meyer, "Henry Clay's Legacy," 478 and n. 15.

355. Vimont, 13.

356. Eric Brooks, curator at Ashland, e-mail of July 24, 2017.

357. Remini, *Henry Clay*, xxi.

358. Meyer, "Henry Clay's Legacy," 479-482.

359. Ibid., 483.

360. Ibid., 487-488. This is about the same time that Dr. Lee Herr came to Lexington with a similar fondness for trotters and the same thoughts about breeding.

361. Ockerman, *Historic Lexington*, 23.

Forgotten Farms

362. Meadowthorpe subdivision website, History, accessed December 22, 2017, http://mnalex.org/history.

363. Trey Crubie, "Historic James Pepper Distillery Fills First Bourbon Barrel Since '58," *Lexington Herald-Leader*, December 22, 2017, 11A, col.1.

364. Peter Brackney, "Kaintuckeean: Meadowthorpe, Lexington's First True Subdivision, Also Site of First Airport," KYForward, accessed December 22, 2017, http://www.kyforward.com/kaintuckeean-meadowthorpe-lexingtons-first-true-subdivision.

365. Knight and Greene, *Country Estates of the Blue Grass*, "The Bell Place," 35.

366. Formally named Tates Creek Road today, the former name, as with almost all roads leading out from Lexington in the nineteenth century, was "Pike," in recognition that the road was a toll road with a turnpike at the tollgate.

367. Merrick Inn, "Our Story," accessed December 22, 2017, http://www.themmerrickinn.com/about-us/our-story.

368. Ibid., 38.

369. Ibid., 42.

370. Ibid., 45.

371. Ibid., 47.

372. Ibid., 56.

373. Ibid., 83.

374. Ibid., 114.

375. *Lexington Herald Leader*, "Standardbreds Gain Prestige at Gainsway," *Bluegrass Review* (January 15, 1950): 36.

376. Dan Liebman, "John Gaines, Formerly Owned Gainesway Farm, Founded Breeders' Cup, Dies at 76," *Bloodhorse Magazine*, February 11, 2005, accessed April 19, 2017, http://bloodhorse.com/horse-racing/articles/171831/john-gaines.

377. "650 Lot Subdivision to be Developed," *Lexington Herald*, July 12, 1957, 1, col. 2.

378. Knight and Greene, *Country Estates of the Blue Grass*, 123.

379. Hollingsworth, *Lexington: Queen of the Bluegrass*, 29.

380. Knight and Greene, *Country Estates of the Blue Grass*, 131.

381. Preston Madden interview, May 16, 2017.

382. Kent Hollingsworth, *Wizard of the Turf*, epilogue by Ray Paulick, following page 134.

383. Madden interview.

384. Kent Hollingsworth, *Wizard of the Turf*, 123.

The Earl of Derby Goes to the Kentucky Derby

385. *Wikipedia*, "Epsom Oaks," accessed January 20, 2018, http://en.wikipedia.org/wiki/Epson_Oaks.

386. Ibid., "Epsom Derby," accessed January 20, 2018, http://en.wikipedia.org/wiki/Epson_Derby.

387. Ibid., "Kentucky Derby," accessed February 18, 2018, https://en.wikipedia.org/wiki/Kentucky_Derby.

388. Ibid., "Thomas Stanley, 1st Earl of Derby," accessed February 18, 2018, https://en.wikipedia/wiki/Thomas_Stanley,_1st_Earl_of_Derby. An announcement appeared in the *Lexington Leader* 445 years later that the Seventeenth Earl of Derby, Edward George Villiers Stanley, would visit Lexington and then go to Louisville for the Kentucky Derby; so far as is known, the first time any of the Derbys came to Kentucky.

389. *Lexington Leader*, March 25, 1930, 6, col. 2

390. *Wikipedia*, "Edward Stanley, 17th Earl of Derby," accessed January 20, 2018, http://en.wikipedia.org/wiki/Edward_Stanley,_17th_Earl_of_Derby.

391. "Derby (17th Earl of) (1865–1948), National Horseracing Museum, accessed January 20, 2018, http://www.horseracinghistory.co.uk/hrho/action/view/Document?id=988.

392. Tony Morris, "A Man Whose Colts Became Basis of the Modern Thoroughbred," *Bloodstock World*, October 1, 2012, 14, accessed January 20, 2018, http://www.racingpost.com.

393. *Lexington Leader*, March 30, 1930, 10, cols. 4–5.

394. Ambrose, *Magnificent Elmendorf*, 99.

395. Ibid., 71.

396. Ibid., 98.

397. *Lexington Leader*, April 8, 1930, 5, col. 1.

398. "Ácquitania," accessed February 18, 2018, www.bryking.com/acuitania/career.html.

399. *Encyclopeadia Britannica*, "Maurentania," http://www.britannica.com/topic/Maurentinia-ship-1906-1935.

400. *Lexington Leader*, May 14, 1930, 1, col. 8.

401. Ibid., May 4, 1939, 1, col. 3.

402. Ibid., May 16, 1930, 1, col. 5.

403. Ibid., May 15, 1930, 1, col. 5.

404. Ibid., May 17, 1930, 1, col. 6.

405. Ibid., May 18, 1930, 1, col. 5.

406. Ibid., May 18, 1939, 1.

407. Ibid., May 18, 1930, 2, col. 5. None of the sources consulted indicate that he ever raced in America.

408. Ibid., May 21, 1930, 1, col. 4, carrying an Associated Press report.

SELECTED BIBLIOGRAPHY

Ambrose, William A., *Kentucky Association (1826–1933)*. Lexington, KY: Limestone Press, 2015.

————. *Magnificent Elmendorf*. Lexington, KY: Limestone Press, 2012.

The Benson and Hedges Book of Racing Colors. Birmingham, UK: Jockey's Association of Great Britain, 1973.

Blackford, Linda B. "Black Fences." *Oxford American* (Spring 2017): 15.

Bolin, James Duane. *Bossism and Reform in a Southern City*. Lexington: University Press of Kentucky, 2000.

Borden, Frederick M. *Silks and Satins*. N.p.: unpublished manuscript, Keeneland Library, Lexington, Kentucky.

Breen, T.H. "Horses and Gentlemen: The Cultural Significance of Gambling among the Gentry of Virginia." *William and Mary Quarterly* (April 1977): 239.

Coleman, J. Winston, Jr. *The Squire's Sketches of Lexington*. Lexington, KY: Henry Clay Press, 1972.

Crews, Ed. "Gambling." *Colonial Williamsburg Journal* (Autumn 2008): 7.

Harison, Lowell H., and James C. Klotter. *A New History of Kentucky*. Lexington: University Press of Kentucky, 1997.

Heidler, David S., and Jeanne T. Heidler. *Henry Clay, The Essential American*. New York: Random House, 2010.

Herbert, Gayle C. *A History of Racing Silks*. Lexington, KY: House of Corrington, 1993.

Hollingsworth, Kent. *The Wizard of the Turf: John E. Madden of Hamburg Place*. N.p.: self-published, 1965. Reprinted by Preston Madden, 1995 and 2000.

Hollingsworth, Randolph. *Lexington: Queen of the Bluegrass*. Charleston, SC: Arcadia Publishing, 2004.

Selected Bibliography

Horse Racing's Top 100 Moments. Lexington, KY: Blood-Horse Publications, 2006.

Hotaling, Edward. *Great Black Jockeys*. New York: Three Rivers Press, 1999.

Keig, Susan Jackson. *Racing Silks and Winning Colors*. N.p.: Beckett Paper Company, 1987.

Kleber, John E., ed. *The Kentucky Encyclopedia*. Lexington: University Press of Kentucky, 1992.

Knight, Thomas A., and Nancy Lewis Greene. *Country Estates of the Blue Grass*. 1903. Reprint, Lexington, KY: Henry Clay Press, 1973.

Mooney, Katherine C. *Race Horse Men*. Cambridge, MA: Harvard University Press, 2014.

Nicholson, James. *The Kentucky Derby: How the Run for the Roses Became America's Premier Sporting Event*. Lexington: University of Kentucky Press, 2014.

Ockerman, Foster, Jr. *Historic Lexington*. San Antonio, TX: HPN Books, 2013.

Perrin, William Henry. *History of Fayette County*. Chicago: O.L. Baskin, 1882.

Phelps, Frank T., et al. *Notable North American Thoroughbreds*. N.p.: Piper Publishing, 1994.

Remini,, Robert V. *Henry Clay, Statesman for the Union*. New York: W.W. Norton, 1991.

Robertson, William H.P. *The History of Horse Racing in America*. New York: Prentice-Hall, 1964.

Simpson, Elizabeth M. *Bluegrass Houses and Their Traditions*. Lexington, KY: Transylvania Press, 1932.

Vosburgh, W.S. *Racing in America 1866–1921*. Lexington, KY: privately printed for the Jockey Club, 1922.

Wall, Mary Jean. *How Kentucky Became Southern*. Lexington: University Press of Kentucky, 2012.

Weeks, Lyman Horace, ed. *The American Turf*. New York: The Historical Company, 1898.

INDEX

About the Author

Foster Ockerman Jr. is a Lexington, Kentucky native and seventh-generation Kentuckian. He is a practicing attorney as well as a historian and the author of five histories including the most recent history of Lexington. His law practice of more than forty years has covered business, real estate, nonprofit organizations, health care and equine law. In addition, he is president and chief historian for the Lexington History Museum, Inc. In 2017, he was historian for the Emmy Award–winning documentary *Belle Brezing & the Gilded Age of Lexington*, and he is host and historian for the new television documentary series *Chronicles—The Kentucky History Magazine.* He is also a USSF-certified soccer referee and a former rock-and-roll disc jockey. He is married to Reverend Martina Ockerman (United Methodist Church), and they have two daughters and a grandson.